Concentric Circles of Concern

Concentric Circles of Concern

W. Oscar Thompson, Jr.

BROADMAN PRESS
Nashville, Tennessee

© Copyright 1981 • Broadman Press
All rights reserved.
4262-33
ISBN: 0-8054-6233-3
Dewey Decimal Classification: 248.5
Subject heading: WITNESSING
Library of Congress Catalog Card Number: 81-67488
Printed in the United States of America

To my daughter,

Damaris

I pray that the words of this book will become reality in your life, and may the words of the Book continually be the word of our God to your heart and life.

Acknowledgments

All of the many wonderful friends who have been a continual source of encouragement in completing the manuscript;

Patsy Kimball and Wanda Hughes, who graciously consented to reading the manuscript;

My secretary, Sara Callaway, who has spent untold hours typing and retyping;

My mother and daddy, who through their love for the Lord taught me the true meaning of relationships;

My family who has loved me and supported me through the years;

My seminary family, my dear students, and all of the gracious churches who have prayed for me, helped me, and encouraged me.

Foreword

When Oscar Thompson had been teaching for a period of a year or so at Southwestern Baptist Theological Seminary, I observed that his classes in personal evangelism were becoming noticeably popular. I knew that students had already come to love Dr. Thompson, but that was not the explanation for their attraction to this particular course. It was something deeper. I investigated and discovered that the concept of "Concentric Circles," which he was teaching, was the magnetic aspect of this course.

Concentric Circles was Oscar's term to describe evangelism which takes place through building and repairing existing personal relationships. This, to him, was the real key to effective personal evangelism. *Relationships* was the big word in his teaching as it had been in his life. As classes began to experiment along the lines they were taught, explosive things began to happen in the lives of students. Some of these you will read about in this book.

This book, in its concepts, is biblical to the core. It encourages a wholesome love of self which frees one in turn to love others and the God who made them like they are.

This book moves one into various circles of relationships with the touch of redeeming love. It was not written *by* an ivory tower theoretician. It was written by a man who lived its message. It is not written *for* ivory tower theoreticians. Its message is one which is to be practiced. The book is destined to be an extremely helpful message for anyone who wants to touch the lives of needy people in this world. I am a better man because I knew well this author. I will be a better man because I have read and will read again this magnificent book.

ROY J. FISH
Professor of Evangelism
Southwestern Baptist Theological Seminary
Fort Worth, Texas

Introduction

This is no ordinary book. Oscar Thompson was no ordinary person. Oscar and I became acquainted almost twenty-five years ago. He was pastoring in a neighboring town. We would often get together and talk of the things of the Lord and pray. I was an observer of his experience of falling in love with Carolyn. I was with him when Damaris was born. When Oscar left the pastorate in Seguin, Texas, to enter the seminary, our opportunities for fellowship were lessened by geographical distance, as well as our busy schedules.

One day I heard that Oscar had cancer. Almost immediately I had a word from the Lord that Oscar would not die but live and declare the works of the Lord (Ps. 118:17). I shared that verse of Scripture with Oscar the morning after the doctors told him that he could not live. He did live! He lived more than four years and declared the works of the Lord to dozens of cancer patients. He preached much in many places to many people. His life was a message of hope and an encouragement to thousands. He did some of the finest work of his young life during those years. I was privileged to share many visits with Oscar during the last months of his life. Morbidity was absent though there was the presence of pain with poor prognosis. I talked with Oscar on Christmas, 1980. He was cheerful and full of praise for a wonderful Christmas. On the Sunday morning after Christmas, 1980, Oscar was called home. His funeral service was a tribute to a holy life and to the glory of God.

As Oscar and I visited during those last days, our conversation often drifted back to the passion of his life, sharing Jesus Christ as Savior and Lord. "To know him and make him known" was a great theme of his life and ministry. It was an ambition realized! *Concentric Circles of Concern,* as a master plan of evangelism, was a subject often discussed. He had delivered these messages on several occasions, always with exciting results and eager hearing.

This work had to be! It will become a standard in the field of endeavoring to reach people for Christ throughout the whole world. It is basic and biblical. You will laugh, be moved to tears, and be filled with joy as you read this volume. It is Oscar through and through! Those who knew him best will know what I mean. Though his wife, Carolyn, has completed the work from the taped messages, Oscar's personality is expressed on every page. His warmth, directness, and disarming sincerity will win your heart. His wit will encourage you. You will thrill to the rich and fresh illustrations of the practicality of the idea of concentric circles in evangelism.

I commend Carolyn for a work well done. I speak a word of appreciation to Sara Callaway for her faithful work with both Oscar and Carolyn to make this work a reality. I congratulate Damaris to whom the book is dedicated and who was the apple of Oscar's eye!

Now I commend this volume to your thorough reading and use. Read it and apply it and your life will never be the same. May God be pleased to give it worldwide use in these strategic days of evangelism.

JACK R. TAYLOR

Contents

1

The Most Important Word

The Word Is Relationship

The most important word in the English language, apart from proper nouns, is *relationship*. You say, but *love* has to be the most important word.

I ask you, though, where is love going if there is no relationship? Relationship is the track. Love is what rolls over the track. Love moves through a relationship. But the thing that satisfies the deepest longing of your being is a relationship with someone.

You may think you want to be a Thoreau and go to Walden Pond. But Thoreau did not stay there forever and neither could you. Why? Because there is something in the nature of people—there is something built into people that desires to be wanted, to be needed, to be fulfilled. Those desires are fulfilled only in relationships.

A little reflection will lead to some obvious but amazing conclusions. First, think on the crisis times of your life:

As a child *separated* from your parents;

As a child *angry* with your parents;

As a teenager *breaking up* with your sweetheart;

The *resentment* and *misunderstanding* that separated you from a friend;

Perhaps the *loss* of a parent or spouse—remember the emptiness, the heartbreak.

Then an *argument* or maybe even *divorce*—with your husband or wife,

The *crisis* with an employee or employer,
Times of *resentment* and *rupture* with family,
Today—the *distress* in business—in your church.

List all the dark, sad, unhappy times in your life and you will
see that the vast majority of these times were created by ruptured
or strained or broken relationships.

Every broken business, every broken home, every broken
friendship is a broken *relationship*. Expand this to city, national,
or international problems, to every crime committed, to every
war from the beginning of time which has brought untold broken
hopes, lives, and dreams resulting from wrong relationships.

Now consider all of the warm wonderful times of joy and
happiness. Do you remember:

The *warm caress* of your parents' arms;

The *giggles* and *laughter* as you romped with your friends or
brothers and sisters in the bright sunshine of a summer afternoon;

The *ecstasy* of your first date with that bright-eyed boy or girl;

The *joy* or a look of *enthusiasm* with those with whom you
work?

All these relationships make you what you are. Right relationships with parents leave you *mentally* and *emotionally* ready
for marriage or for a baby brought into the family—new relationships.

The special days of happiness—birthday, anniversary,
Thanksgiving, Christmas—are fulfilling because of warm, wonderful relationships.

As human history so painfully demonstrates, bad relationships produce:

> broken marriages
> broken homes
> unsuccessful businesses
> divided churches
> weak governments
> chaotic nations

Solve the relationship problems and there would be no divorce, no war, no employer-employee or labor-management disputes. Solve the relationship problems of the world and humanity's most perplexing problems are solved since right relationships produce:

> solid marriages
> stable homes
> successful businesses
> ministering churches
> good governments
> strong nations

When society *ceases* to treasure relationships, it becomes decadent. Manners become course and cheap. Common courtesy is soon forgotten. Hearts become thankless, ceasing to show appreciation.

Dear friend, if your life is in turmoil today, I venture to say it is because of a ruptured relationship with someone. The purpose of this book is to explore what may be the causes of your broken relationships and show how they can be mended. In other words, it is written to help *meet* your *needs*.

The Two Basic Relationships in Life

There are two basic relationships in life. One, of course, is the vertical relationship with the Father. The other is the horizontal relationship that we have with other people. When a person establishes by faith the proper vertical relationship with the Father, the person is then able to have right horizontal relationships with others and deal with the basic problems of the world.

If you solve the relationship problems at home, you have solved problems between husband and wife, parents and children, brothers and sisters. The home is the context in which God has placed us to teach us how to have right relationships. To a large degree, the reason the world is coming unglued is because our best school for teaching relationships, the home, is not teaching correctly.

I boarded a plane bound for San Francisco one December
and found my seat. Sitting on my left was a professor from the
University of Texas, a deacon from one of the churches in Austin
and a delightful fellow. We talked for a few moments.

On my right was a man who seemed very busy trying to get
some writing done. I did not bother him. He was a Hollywood
producer. We just greeted each other. I knew I had three hours
with him. He was not going anywhere, not for three hours anyway. After a time he put his pen down, and we began talking. He
asked, "What do you do?" I long since have learned not to tell
people I am a Baptist preacher, especially if I am on a three-hour
flight. They may just have a horror spell right there and jump!

Instead I replied, "Well, I am a teacher." Then I waited.

He asked, "What do you teach?" Do you want me to say
that I told him I teach evangelism at a theological seminary? No! I
was not going to do that either.

So I continued, "That is interesting you should ask. What I
basically teach is that the most important word in the English language is *relationship*. If we can solve the relationship problems in
this world, we have solved domestic problems, neighbor problems, city problems, and international problems."

Well, he looked out the window and thought for a moment;
and then he said, "Hey, that is right!" Then I picked up a copy of
Time and started reading.

But he persisted, "Is that all you are going to tell me?"

"You want to know more?" And so I began. I said to him
exactly what I am going to explain to you in this book. I
explained that there are two types of relationships. There are
horizontal relationships with people. Then there is the vertical
relationship with the Creator of the universe who has laid down
the basis for all of our other relationships. We are made by his
design. If we follow his design, things work. If we do not follow
his design, things do not work. Because man basically has not
followed God's design, relationships are not working very well.

Fortunately for us, however, God has also given us a plan to reestablish those relationships. I told the man on the plane, "It is best seen in the teaching of Jesus Christ."

"Oh!" he said, "I have read the Bible. I agree with many things that Jesus said. Now, I do not believe everything the Bible says, but . . ."

"Well, that is what I teach." If I had been flying to Houston in only forty-five minutes, I would not have been so free with my time. But this was a three-hour flight. I went back to reading *Time*. And he just sort of hung there. I read for awhile.

"Tell me some more," the producer said.

I thought to myself, *Glad you asked*. Well, to make a long story short, we talked for a long time during that flight. The man had many problems with the Scriptures. But you and I know that many people in the secular world have rejected the Scriptures because they have heard only a caricature, not because they know anything about them.

I maintain that most people have not rejected Jesus Christ. They merely reject a caricature of him. They have rejected "churchianity." But they have not basically rejected Jesus Christ because they have never really heard about him. That is the tragedy. The producer and I talked about that, then we talked about the person of Jesus Christ.

"Well, how do you know who he is and what he is?" the man asked.

I went through that simple answer that Jesus either was who he said he was or he was psychotic or he was a great fraud. "Dick," I said, "you are going to have to decide ultimately who he is on the basis of the evidence. You cannot just conclude that Jesus was the greatest teacher that ever lived. You see, this great teacher said, 'I am God.' And no great teacher is a falsifier. You are either going to have to take Jesus at his word or reject him." Then I went back to reading *Time*.

My deacon friend in the next seat was praying for me. Finally, as we flew over El Capitan, the captain said, "There is Yosemite." We looked out, and I knew that time was running out. I really began to pray. "Father, oh, Father, I cannot convince this fellow." He was having all kinds of trouble in relationships with his workers, as well as with his family. He was trying to get his family back together and was frantic.

The latter part of that flight, as we crossed the mountains before circling the bay area, I saw tears forming in his eyes as he looked out the window. Then he turned to me and said, "Oscar, this morning I got down on my knees in a motel room in Dallas. I prayed, 'Dear God, if there is a God, I have to have help. Please send somebody.' " He reached over and took me by my elbow and said, "God sent you. Now what do I do?"

"The first thing that you are going to have to do is surrender to the absolute authority of Jesus Christ and let him be the Master of your life. You are going to have to accept his conditions for coming to God. You cannot come on your own conditions.

"Dick, if you read the biography of every great Christian in history, you would find something very interesting. George Whitefield, John Wesley, Martin Luther, many great Christians whom history says were great men of God intensely struggled with God as they searched for him. All of them had one basic problem. Though they were seeking God with all their hearts, they were seeking him on their conditions. Only when they abandoned their conditions in coming to God did God accept them. When each one finally gave up and said, 'I will accept your conditions, whatever they are and whatever they cost me,' then instantly, immediately, God revealed himself."

Dear reader, I do not know who you are, but I want you to know that the first step, the very first step in coming to know God intimately in a personal relationship, is coming on his conditions. We have to accept those conditions every day. Colossians 2:6 says, "As you therefore have received Christ Jesus the Lord, so walk in Him." Now what does that mean? It means that as we accepted Jesus Christ by faith, we walk with him each day by faith.

Now, Amos 3:3 asked, "Can two walk together, except they be agreed?" (KJV). If they be agreed, then it means that I have to come back and accept God's conditions in total agreement with him for the unfolding of that walk. Then, if we do that, the Lord says, "I will reveal myself in your life."

Having accepted God's conditions in establishing a relationship with him, we then must accept his conditions for establishing horizontal relationships with people.

As Dick got off the plane, he looked over and said, "Thank you, Oscar. I have needed this all my life."

Discovering the Plan

Before teaching at the seminary, I preached for twenty-four years and pastored for about twenty years. Most of the concepts of evangelism that I had read stressed training people to tell Person X about the Lord.

As I began to prepare to teach at Southwestern, I did not take my position lightly. I was very aware of James's admonition, "Let not many of you become teachers, my brethren, knowing that as such we shall incur a stricter judgment" (Jas. 3:1). So I realized, to whom much is given, much is required.

In one year, I teach over one thousand students. Those students will literally go to the ends of the earth to carry the gospel. So I prayed, "Father, teach me first so that I may teach them." If you are going to teach or preach, do not teach concepts. Those are just head knowledge; teach life-style. You have already lived it. You know it will work. Teach life-style. You can never lead anyone closer to the Lord than you are. Evangelism must flow out of a life. It is not something you can learn in a textbook, take tests over, and make *A*'s on to be assured of success. When you get out into the world, if it is not life-style, you will flunk the course. Your life-style should reveal what you are.

The second thing I did was to commit myself to read through the New Testament once a month, looking for strategy. We are always looking for new types of plans. Everyone in education, every pastor is always looking for fresh, new ways of doing things. Variety is the spice of life. It really is. You do not want to do everything the same old way. But you want to do everything in a biblical way. How did they do it in the New Testament? As I studied the New Testament, I looked for a strategy, an idea. Finally, I began to see it rise like fog in the morning above a forest. At first, it was almost imperceptible. Then all at once it became clear. It was there all the time! I just had not seen it. The most important word in the English language is *relationship*. The gospel always moved on lines of relationship—Jerusalem, Judea, Samaria, the uttermost parts of the earth—in seemingly out-moving waves.

Formulating the Plan

Acts 20:20 says that they went "from house to house." Andrew went to Peter; Philip, to Nathaniel; the woman at the well, back to her city. Cornelius went to his household; the Philippian jailer, to his household; the wild man of the Gadarenes sitting in the boat clothed and in his right mind, with Jesus telling him to go home to his friends to tell them what great things the Lord had done for him.

If you read through the whole New Testament, you will see it. It is nothing profound, but it is just as natural as anything can possibly be. If something is genuine in my life and your life, the natural thing to want to do is to share it with those we know. Now, isn't that reasonable to assume? It seemed we were always training people in evangelism to go to Person X out there somewhere. But there is no prior relationship established with Person X. Life-style evangelism in the New Testament did not begin with Person X. It worked through relationships that had already been established.

Presenting the Plan

When the concept of life-style evangelism first began to roll over in my mind, I had been asked to teach an evangelism class for a couple of nights for a friend at a Bible institute. As I drove to class that first night, I kept mulling over this concept in my mind. I got to the class. As I was thinking through this concept, I drew

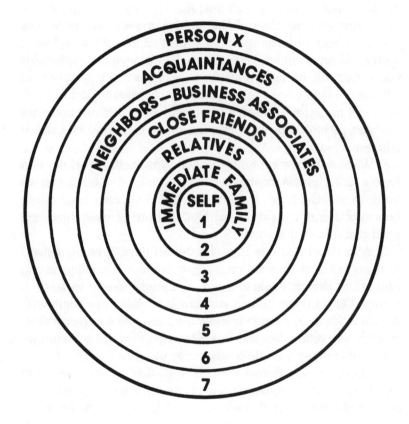

seven circles on the board. They were like a target with a bull's
eye in the center, Concentric Circles. Circle 1 is Self. Circle 2 is
Immediate Family. Circle 3 is Relatives. Circle 4 is Close Friends.
Circle 5 is Business Associates and Neighbors. Circle 6 is
Acquaintances. Circle 7 is Person X.

I said to my class, "The gospel moves on contiguous
lines—on lines of relationship." I explained the circles and what
each circle represented. "Now," I said, "I believe that God holds
you responsible for everyone whom he brings into your sphere of
influence. Many of us come to study evangelism to go from Circle 1 out to Circle 7 to salve our consciences because there are
ruptured relationships in Circles 2 through 6 that we had rather
skip over."

When we have ruptured relationships horizontally, we also
have a ruptured relationship vertically, with God. It is not that we
do not know the Lord. It is just that he is not really Lord of our
lives. We are not willing to let him be Lord of everything and
accept people on his conditions.

With Person X, our life-styles do not have to be consistent.
We can talk and then be on our way. There is nothing wrong
with telling Person X about Jesus. We are supposed to do that.
God will bring these people into our lives; but if we cannot tell
people in Circle 2 through 6 about the Lord, we are hypocritical.
We are play acting. We are unreal people. If we are genuine, we
will want to share with those closest to us.

I have preached long enough to be able to read people in
the congregation. I have noticed children in a service watching a
June bug climb up and down a wall. I know they heard every
word I said. They were thinking.

I have watched other people who sit there piously. They
would look straight at me and yet would be looking straight
through me. I know when they are listening. I know when they
are hurting.

As I spoke to that class, I noticed a lady sitting on the back
row. I watched her face distort. She was hurting. She was either

having a gall bladder attack or I was saying something that was hurting her. It was the latter. She left very quickly that night, not knowing that she would have to put up with me again.

I came back the next week. She was not expecting me. She looked up and said, "Oh, you again!" That always warms your heart. She sat down and said, "I want to see you after class."

Wow! I had not been talked to like that since the second grade when I used to. . . . I won't tell you what I did.

Afterward she came to my desk and said, "You hurt me last week."

I said, "Dear heart, I do not understand."

"You said that I came here to study to tell Person X about the Lord." She had *personalized* it. She had *internalized* it. She continued, "You see, I was estranged from my husband and my two sons. It was not their fault. It was mine. I came here to salve my conscience. After last week, the Holy Spirit took hold of me. I knew I must go home."

As she wept, she said, "I want you to know that I have accepted Jesus Christ's conditions for reconciliation. You see, my conditions would never have reconciled us. I had to accept Jesus Christ's conditions."

Please understand this. You may accept another person's conditions or you may go with your conditions to establish a relationship, but it will never be a lasting relationship until you accept Jesus Christ's conditions. Why? Because that is the way you are designed.

She wept and said, "I am back at home now. But do you know what has happened? The timidity that I have always had toward Person X is gone. When Jesus became Lord of my relationships, he took away my timidity."

I said, "Glory! That's it—*relationships!*"

Living Proof

I went back to my own class at the seminary the next day. My dear students never know what is going to happen next. I

said, "Scratch everything; we are starting over." Well, we were
halfway through the semester. They looked at me like a calf
looks at a new gate.

I continued by saying, "Class, I have a new assignment. It is
an assignment that you cannot finish this semester. You will not
finish it until God takes you home."

I drew those Concentric Circles and said, "The gospel did
not go from house to house to house to house down the street,
like a nice, neat census. It went from house to house to house to
house:

"God holds you responsible for *every* person who comes
into your spheres of influence—into your Concentric Circles.
There are people in all of your circles whom you touch every
day, and you do not even see them. Some of them are cantankerous, some of them you do not like, and some of them you
really do not want to love; but they are there. They are there for
you to love—to meet their needs—to draw to Jesus.

"How many of you have loved ones whom you are not sure
know the Lord? How many of you have come to seminary to
learn only how to go and tell Person X about the Lord?"

Just as I was going to continue, a young man on my left
blurted out, "Dr. Thompson, I have all kinds of problems with
that!"

I turned and said, "What's the matter, Jim?"

The impact of the moment had overwhelmed him. The
assignment had touched an area of bitterness in his life that he
did not know how to deal with. He said, "You do not understand! You grew up in a Christian home. But my father abandoned my mother and me twenty-six-and-a-half years ago. I am
twenty-seven-years old. I have never seen him. I DO NOT
WANT TO SEE HIM!"

I whispered, "Oh." A class of sixty. He did not realize what
had happened to him. All that pent-up anger just rolled out.

Gently, I turned to the board. Speaking silently to the Lord,
I said, "Lord Jesus, love Jim through me. Please *meet* his *need*."

The gospel did not go from house to house to house to house like a nice, neat census down the street.

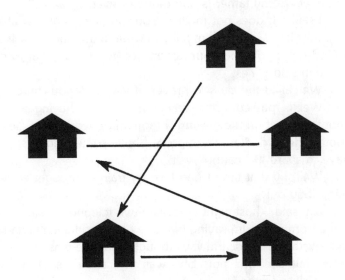

It went from house to house to house to house.

A passage of Scripture came to mind. I wrote on the board Matthew 6:14-15. My translation was, "Because of the love of Jesus and his forgiveness in my life, I must be ready to forgive if I am to be forgiven."

I said, "In other words you do not give people what they *deserve*. You give them what they *need*."

I turned back around and the Holy Spirit was doing his work. I said, "Jim, I think that you are in this class through divine providence. I think God is going to teach me something and you something and this class something. For if I cannot forgive another on the grounds of God's infinite grace, then God is going to have great difficulty forgiving me (Matt. 6:14-15). Your father does not deserve forgiveness, but neither do you and neither do I."

Tears were trickling down Jim's cheeks. The Holy Spirit descended upon that class. Jim said, "What must I do? I do not know where my father is. He may not even be alive."

I said, "It does not matter. Your problem is one of attitude. You take it to God, let him tell you what to do, and leave it there. If God helps you find your father, you will know what to do."

Jim said, "Yes."

We called the class to prayer. It was a glorious time.

Weeks passed. One day Jim came sashaying into class about two feet off the ground. I thought he worked for Bell Helicopter. He said, "Dr. Thompson, I have something to say. I just have to share it. I cannot wait!"

Well, by that time I had lost my train of thought anyway. I said, "Say on!"

Jim said, "Last night I received two telephone calls. The first came from my mom saying that one of my godly aunts had gone to be with the Lord. I always thought that she was my mother's sister, but she was not. She was my father's sister who had stayed close to the family.

"At 11:00 I received a second call, and the voice on the other end said, 'Jim? Son? . . . although I have no right to call you son. But I have heard that you are at Southwestern Seminary preparing for the ministry. I thought you would like to know that recently I gave my life to Jesus Christ. Can you forgive me for what I have done? ' "

Jim said, "When I could quit sobbing, we talked. We spent an hour on the phone. My father said, 'Son, may I come to your graduation? ' "

In May of that year, we were marching in the processional of the graduation exercise in all our academic regalia. You look more like Zorro than anything else. Well, someone grabbed me out of the line. It was Jim.

He took me over to a little man who looked up through his trifocals. In tears, Jim said, "Dr. Thompson, this is my father. Dad, this is my professor."

What do you say? We just sort of went into a three cornered hug. That, dear friend, is the gospel of Jesus Christ.

If there are ruptured relationships between you and those in your Concentric Circles, there is going to be a rupture of the flow of the Holy Spirit through your life.

Jesus put it very plainly in Matthew 5:23-24. He taught us to confess wrong relationships and make them right before coming to worship the Father.

I believe with all my heart that when you have to dig deep into the well to get the water flowing, there is something wrong in a relationship somewhere. When relationships are right, the flow of the Holy Spirit is like an artesian well that bursts up and out and over! All of our training for evangelism will be less useful until we make those relationships right.

2
Discovering and Liking the Real You

Let's discuss Circle 1, Self, and what keeps the divine flow moving through it. No matter what methodology we use, if self is not right, we have problems. Self is your biggest problem and my biggest problem. In the natural economy of the self, we say, "I love *me,* and I want *you* to make *me* happy." Isn't that nice? As long as you meet *my* conditions, everything is going to be all

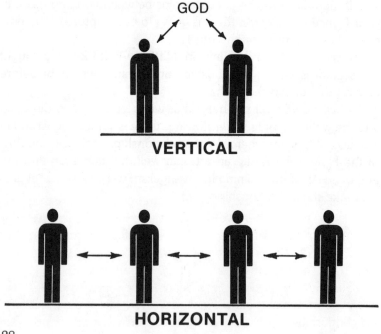

VERTICAL

HORIZONTAL

right. The only problem with that is that it will not work! There are two basic relationships in life. One is the horizontal relationship that we have with other people. But the most important relationship we have is with the Father. He has laid down the basis for all of our other relationships. The *only* way any of us can come to the Father is on the Father's conditions. Accepting his conditions for relationships means that we forfeit forever the right to choose whom we love. The kind of love we will express has nothing to do with looks, age, shape, size, color, race, sweetness, hostility, or personality. Anyone Jesus chooses, we will love.

In relationships—marriage, business, or any interpersonal relationship with anyone—we must accept Jesus' lordship. When Jesus becomes Lord of our lives, he is going to draw people into our circles who will not be lovely. Jesus said that any sinner can love any other sinner. You love me; I'll love you. You don't love me; I won't love you. We become a mutual admiration society.

Implosion or Explosion

Have you ever been in churches that have become mutual admiration societies? People who have needs band together. They find a solitude and a comfort in having their own needs met. Then, instead of becoming an *explosion* when their needs have been met, they become cliquish and have an *implosion*.

Do you know what an implosion is? An implosion explodes within and then just consumes. It is just debris. Have you ever seen that happen in a church? We begin to love one another and there is no threat. Then we feel threatened when someone new tries to enter our "safe little world." The reason many churches never make it is because they become mutual admiration societies. They "preach the Word" but never reach anybody.

Sunday School classes can become the same way. You see, when we are threatened and not really sure about ourselves, we feel comfortable only with our friends. Consequently, we do not want strangers coming in and monkeying with our security.

Now, dear friend, God's plan for the church was not to stay in Jerusalem. Likewise it is *not* just Jerusalem that we are responsible for. What happened to those believers who stayed in Jerusalem for twelve years, not doing what Jesus told them to do? The fire fell! Persecution hit! You may read through the Book of Acts and think they went everywhere. Well, they went everywhere for awhile. There were some scattered fires, but then they became self-inclusive, the Jews particularly. They imploded instead of exploding. That will happen to you if you do not know God's design for your life.

Understanding the Body

Ephesians 4, Romans 12, and 1 Corinthians 12 talk about gifts of the body of Christ, the church. The God-given gift of administration enables a person to recognize a situation and have control over it. I do not have the gift of administration. I could not organize my way out of a brown paper bag. But, I do have the gift of mercy. That is my spiritual gift, and I am a pastor-teacher. I know what my gifts are. I do not apologize for them. I can walk into a room and within thirty minutes can tell you the people who are hurting. Some of you also have the gift of mercy. Others of you have the gift of administration. We are to work as a body under the headship of Christ to draw the world to himself. My gift is not your gift. Do not desire my gift. God's sovereignty gives the gift. Do not start asking God for some specific spiritual gift. He knows what he wants to do with you, and he knows where you fit into the body.

Suppose you are a toe and you say, "Lord, I want to be an eye. God, I just have to be an eye. I want the gift of being an eye."

The Lord says, "No, I made you a toe."

"Lord, I want to be an eye."

"OK, you can be an eye, but the only thing you are ever going to see is the inside of a sock."

We need to recognize our spiritual gifts and use them to build up the body of Christ. This brings us back to loving people—meeting their needs. How can we love someone that we have never learned to understand? If Jesus dwells in you and in someone else, it is absurd to say you have a personality clash with that person. Many times these so-called clashes come when two people do not understand their spiritual gifts and how they fit into the body of Christ, the church.

In other words, try to look at the other person from God's point of view. Understand how the other person is to function in the body. If you understand that, you will then be able to understand his actions. If you have the gift of mercy and someone else the gift of prophecy, in order to accept each other, you are going to have to understand how each of you fit in God's plan for the church.

The Design for Me

Let's talk about Circle 1, Self. We are designed for fellowship with the King. Like the bird was made for the air and the fish was made for the sea, people were created for *fellowship* with God. Nothing, but nothing, is going to satisfy the deepest needs of our being until we have fellowship with him, which in turn will result in fellowship with others on his conditions.

The Unreal Person

We learn about relationships first in the home. We can play games when we are at school and at work and so on. We can *wear* our *masks* with people. But we are always changing our masks. With one person we are a certain way, with another person we are a certain way, and in business we are a certain way. We feel we have to be a certain way if we want to elicit a specific type of response from a client or an employer or employee. Consequently, we wear these masks and after awhile we forget which mask we have worn with what person. Suddenly we do a switch and they think, *Wow!* Have you ever done that?

Now do not sit there and look so pious. I know better. See, that is our problem. How can we develop a relationship with an unreal person?

Feeling Good About You

First of all, God wants *you* to feel *good* about *you*. The Scriptures say, "You shall love your neighbor as yourself" (Matt. 19:19). You *cannot* love others without loving yourself. You have to feel good about you.

Because of my work with cancer patients and my ministry to people in working with stress, I had the opportunity to lecture at Harvard University in their department of psychology in the area of stress. This is what I told them: "I am by trade an academician, but this morning I do not want to be an academician. I just want to invite you into my own vulnerability, into my own experience with cancer. I want to tell you my story. My purpose for being here is not to come up with a scientific treatise but to meet needs in your life . . in other words, I want to love you."

I continued, "I want to love you, and I want to meet needs in your life. Someone in your family, or someone that you touch, or perhaps even you, may someday have cancer." Then I told them about the person of Jesus Christ as the center of life and how he has designed us and also how stress affects the human body.

After I spoke, a number of people lined up to speak to me. Many said, "We have not heard this about the person of Christ." You see, most intellectuals have *never* heard a clear presentation of the gospel, the real story about Jesus Christ. So do not be intimidated by people in the academic world or the secular world. They hurt just like everybody else. Go ahead and love them. Do not be concerned about what they think of you.

God wants you to feel good about you. He wants you to love you. That sounds strange, doesn't it? What do you do when you love you? In Ephesians, the Bible tells husbands to love their wives as they love their own bodies (5:28). Do you stand in front of the mirror and say, "Oh, I just love me"? No! You do not get goose pimplish over looking at yourself in the mirror. If you do, you have a problem.

What you do when you love yourself is to meet your own needs. You feed yourself, cleanse yourself, brush yourself, shine yourself, paint yourself, clothe yourself, warm yourself, and cool yourself. Is there anything wrong with any of those things? Of course not. That is loving yourself. God wants us to take care of ourselves. Love is meeting needs.

As we mature, we take on a family and God teaches us how to meet one another's needs. That is the reason God gave mothers and fathers babies. In the home, people learn how the Holy Father works so that they can meet the needs of little ones. As those little ones have their needs met, they know they are loved.

You and Your Inferiority Complex

As pastor consultant for the Cancer Research and Counseling Foundation, I once spoke at a medical convention. I was talking about stress and its effects when I commented: "According to an industrial psychologist, 95 percent of the people, by the time they are six years old, have inferiority complexes. They are not sure about themselves." One of my colleagues stopped me. He told me that I was wrong. That always makes a person feel good! He said, "It is not 95 percent. It is 100 percent! Every child by the time he is six years old has an inferiority complex." This is probably so.

As a child grows up, he says, "How do I feel about me?" A child may take a number of approaches. He may be aggressive, and adults conclude that he feels secure in himself. He knows who he is. He is all right. Often that is nothing more than his trying to get attention because he is not sure of himself.

Then on the flip side is the child who becomes a wallflower and is afraid to say anything. He is shy. I am taking into consideration the various types of personalities. Now, we make so many

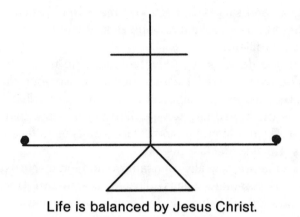

Life is balanced by Jesus Christ.

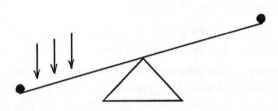

Pressures and problems push down on us.

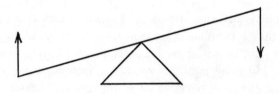

Old nature uses wrong ways to get back up.

mistakes in judging a Christian's life. We meet this gang buster fellow who is a salesman and could sell snow cones to the Eskimos. We say, "Boy, if he were ever saved, he would really be great." Maybe he would and maybe he would not. Do not think that aggressiveness is necessarily spirituality. Some of the most passive people and passive types of personalities are very secure in themselves and are great channels of love. We do not see them, but oh, how God uses them.

Remember another thing. When you are converted, God *does not* change your *personality*. He changes your *character*. There is a vast difference. He wants you to be you. But he wants to be Christ in you. He wants to reach out through you.

All of us, you see, were born with the first Adam's nature. Its allegiance has three words, all personal pronouns: *me, my,* and *mine.* We carry this nature into business. Get all you can, can all you get, sit on the can, and do not share it with anybody else. It is just me, my, mine. That is the old Adamic nature.

We Need to Be Balanced

But the *self* seeks balance. Our lives are much like a seesaw. The *balance* represents you. It represents me. The problems of life come, and *pressure pushes* us *down* to make us think less of ourselves. We feel guilty, and this pushes the old Adamic nature further *down.* But that old Adamic nature wants to get back *up.*

All this begins to happen at an early age. *All* we want is to be *balanced,* but someone else gets on our little seesaw and begins to criticize us, to push us back down. Any kind of criticism causes our immediate reaction. What do we do? If you hit me, I am going to do what? I am going to hit you back! You criticize me, and I am going to say that you are not so hot either. This is the natural, normal result of self-compensation—I am going to take care of me.

When someone tries to help us, we are sensitive and insecure. We think others are *pushing* us *down;* so then we work to *push* ourselves back *up* again. I am not trying to be psychological. I am trying to be biblical. Then, when we begin to react toward other people, we begin to sense a feeling of control. If we have natural abilities, we use that control for ourselves.

Why Do We Intimidate?

But the aggressive person with a deep inferiority complex must dominate everybody else and run the show. He intimidates others in the church, in the family, or in business because that makes him feel good about himself.

Many little country churches get into a family hierarchical structure. They become the only place some people can have authority. But God never gets the glory, and these people hurt all their days, trying to suck the juices out of the situation just to run the show. Isn't that tragic?

There are things that push us down. One of the things that pushes us down is guilt.

There are two types of guilt. There is *real guilt* and that is the guilt before God. I have sinned against the Lord. I have broken his laws; I have been self-centered. This is real guilt. The other is self-imposed guilt.

You can receive forgiveness for real guilt, but you cannot receive forgiveness for self-imposed guilt. Some of you have let God forgive you, but you have never forgiven yourself. Consequently, you are not sure that God has forgiven you. So you hurt.

With this self-imposed guilt pressing us down, we make our plans; but they come unglued. We put all of our eggs into one basket, but all of a sudden that basket comes apart. Then all we have is egg shells. We invest our lives in things, and in the end there is nothing. Why? Here is what I tell my young preachers.

The Achiever

One thing we might try is achievement. If I have achievement, it will *pull* me back *up* and help me feel *balanced*. If I am an achiever, people will not criticize me. They will praise me, and that praise will *lift* me *up*. So I must become an achiever.

Nothing is wrong with achievement. You were designed to be an achiever. You were designed for accomplishment. But read very carefully. *Why* are you to accomplish? To glorify God. But most of us want to achieve so that we can feel good about ourselves. I want to feel so good about me that I can raise myself *up* and look above my peers. Now I am a little higher; so I can look down on other people. Have you ever done that?

I really try to rattle the cage of my young preachers about this. I say, "You fellows go out into the association. You try to baptize more people, raise more money, build more buildings, and do all of these things. Because you have great native ability, you do them. You are so proud. You have done a good job. But you have done it for the wrong motivation. When you stand before God, it is not going to be gold, silver, and precious stones; it is going to be hay, wood, and stubble."

Many of us serve God out of a guilty conscience. Our pastor tells us that we need to witness and we need to serve. We have guilty consciences. We have not served God; so we get busy in the church and work so that we can get status and can feel good about ourselves. Have you ever seen that syndrome? What is the problem with all of this?

Some people go out into the business world. Some people go out in the academic world. Some people go out—! I have seen fellows work on doctor's degrees just so that they could be called "doctor." The only reason they wanted a doctor's degree was for status, so that they could feel good about themselves, and not to gain credentials to work in a place where God could put them.

I want you to read about an achiever in Ecclesiastes 2:1-11. What a pessimistic fellow! Listen to his conclusions regarding his achievements:

I said to myself, "Come now, I will test you with pleasure. So enjoy yourself." And behold, it too was futility. I said of laughter, "It is mad-

ness," and of pleasure, "What does it accomplish?" I explored with my
mind how to stimulate my body with wine while my mind was guiding
me wisely, and how to take hold of folly, until I could see what good
there is for the sons of men to do under heaven the few years of their
lives. I enlarged my works: I built houses for myself, I planted vineyards
for myself; I made gardens and parks for myself, and I planted in them
all kinds of fruit trees; I made ponds of water for myself from which to
irrigate a forest of growing trees. I bought male and female slaves, and I
had homeborn slaves. Also I possessed flocks and herds larger than all
who preceded me in Jerusalem. Also, I collected for myself silver and
gold, and the treasure of kings and provinces. I provided for myself
male and female singers and the pleasures of men—many concubines.
Then I became great and increased more than all who preceded me in
Jerusalem. My wisdom also stood by me. And all that my eyes desired I
did not refuse them. I did not withhold my heart from any pleasure, for
my heart was pleased because of all my labor and this was my reward
for all my labor.

This guy had "I" trouble. He had VISA, MasterCard, Carte
Blanche. He had a blank check, no limit. You say, "Wouldn't
that be great?" Not necessarily. Listen to more: "Thus I consid-
ered all my activities which my hands had done and the labor
which I had exerted, and behold all was vanity and striving after
wind and there was no profit under the sun."

Well, should he never have done those things? No! But you
see, he wanted them for the wrong reason: I, me, my, mine.
Crunch! You say, "What does all of this have to do with evangelism?" Everything. Because you see there is a flow of life in every
life. The flow is either through you or to you. Jesus told us that
out of our "innermost being shall flow rivers of living water"
(John 7:38). But you see, the flow cannot flow through you
when you are wanting it always to flow to you. We are not going
to win the world when we are not sure about our own world.

An Artificial World

Another thing a person might do is to create for himself an
artificial world. This can be done in a number of ways. If he does

not like his world, then he begins to daydream. The psychologists used to call it neurosis.

All of us are a little neurotic. All the world is peculiar except me and thee, and sometimes I think thou are a bit peculiar too! So we begin to daydream.

It is all right to build air castles, just do not move into them. In reality then you begin to back off and move into psychosis. I have seen people retreat. They back off from life. They cannot take it.

Another way a person creates an artificial life-style is that he begins to say, "I do not like the way I am; I do not feel good about me." He cannot face himself, so he begins to daydream.

Alcohol becomes an escape mechanism for some people. They drink because they are exhausted from the pressures of the day. "I'll have a cool one; it will relax my nerves." Instead, alcohol becomes an escape mechanism because escapees do not know how to get back.

Still another way to create an artificial world is through the drug culture. It is the same song, but the second verse. Taking drugs is only a person running from the reality of saying, "I must be balanced."

I'm Just One Beggar Telling Another

Now, do not throw rocks at people who hurt. You see, the problem in our world is that we have judged all these folk. Do not go to another man who is caught in sin with an attitude of, "I am holy and look at me." All you are trying to do is give yourself undue praise. But I will show you a *spiritual man*. Read Galations 6:1, *"Brethren, even if a man is caught in any trespass, you who are spiritual, restore such a one in a spirit of gentleness; each one looking to yourself, lest you too be tempted."* If you find a spiritual Christian, you will see someone who is reaching out to a man saying, "Look, brother, *I am* just one beggar telling *another* beggar where we can both find bread." That is meeting needs. There is the *holiness* of God.

The essence of this whole thing is that God says, "You

restore one; you reach out." There go I except by the grace of God. Isn't that right? That is when a church begins to *explode* rather than *implode*. We begin to reach out. We begin to love. We begin to meet needs all around us. That is the key.

The reason our teenagers get started on drugs, fall into sexual immorality, and all these other things they do is because of that inferiority complex. Why? Because they want to be accepted. They want to feel good about themselves. If they do not know who they are, if they are not balanced, they are dependent upon the acceptance of their peer group. So they yield to the peer group. A guy who feels good about himself does not need to go along with the crowd.

Some kids say, "I do not want to be a holy Joe. I want to go through high school and have the kids like me without surrendering my Christian testimony, but how do I deal with that bunch?" The answer is very simple. Just say, "Look, you want me to smoke a joint with you? I want to thank you for wanting to include me in your group. That means so much to me, but let me tell you something. If I do that, I am going to hurt somebody I love very, very much. If you genuinely want me to be your friend and want to include me, you do not want me to hurt somebody that I love very much, do you?"

See, put the ball in their court without condemning them. I have had teenager after teenager come back and say, "Hey, that works." You do not isolate. You do not condemn them. You just reach out to them and say, "I have somebody I do not want to hurt." Doing this makes a difference.

The "Topped Out"

Now the problem with achievement is that a person can climb the ladder. Most people never top out, and there are some relatively happy people who live all of their lives and are successful in that they have homes and cars and families. They raise a good family with moderate success, and they are not religious. We see the exterior of their lives.

Most people are so busy climbing that they do not know if they are happy or not. Sometimes a man is so busy making a business he forgets his family obligations. As one old preacher used to say, "Some fellows are so concerned about white-faced cows that they have completely forgotten about their white-faced boys." They are concerned about things rather than God. Why? Because they are not balanced.

Nothing is wrong with achievement. God wants us to achieve. He wants us to be the best businessmen we can be, the best teachers, or the best anything. That is fine.

But why? The achievement syndrome may top out, and many of the people do top out. Hemingway did. He was the top writer in the world, had married several times and lived as he pleased. One writer said of him ten years before his death, "Here is the man who has broken all the laws and proved that sin does pay." But, three years before his death he lost three-quarters of his mental ability and ended up blowing his brains out. A Monroe, a Garland—you name them—they topped out from boredom. So after a person has done all there is to do and he tops out, where is he going? There is no place to go. He is still looking for achievement, but it is not there.

The "Bottomed Out"

This is where we find so many people in our affluent society. We have the two extremes, do we not? We have people topping out. We have people bottoming out; and both extremes say, "I do not want to live any more." These are the suicidal tendencies.

The Real You

How do we achieve balance? This is an oversimplification, but here it is. When someone blames me, what do I do to *push me up?* If I know Jesus Christ, I take this blame to the cross. I can say, "OK Lord Jesus, thank you so much for loving me." If this person is right, you go to that person and say, "You are exactly right. I am a clod. I did say something wrong. Will you forgive

me?" Then go to the cross. Then I am clear and clean and
balanced and do not have a running battle with anyone or ruptured relationships anywhere. Remember, if we are going to
come to the *balance* that Jesus offers, we must come to the
cross; die to self; to me, my, and mine; and let him be Lord.

Then even if someone does blame us and even if we are *not*
guilty, we take that to the cross. We do not let bitterness build up.

You say, "But he criticizes me all the time." Well, so what? If
you know who you are, who cares? The person who is balanced
is not devastated by criticism. He knows who he is.

You have to remember that when you start living a holy life
and God begins to love through you, people are going to be
upset because your life-style is going to rise higher than their life-
styles. Your life-style condemns theirs. They will start throwing
rocks. People will say, "What is this?" But you just love them
without saying, "Yes, I am pretty holy, aren't I?" As Spurgeon
said, "We always thought this brother was humble until one day
he told us he was."

Why do you achieve? Why do you want to make straight
A's in school? God made you to be the *best* you can be; so do
not feel guilty. Do not *compare* yourself with anyone else. You
are like a snowflake. You are like a fingerprint. You are you.
You are not to compare yourself with anyone else. You are one
of a kind. God made you to be you.

Some preachers are always comparing themselves with
other preachers. But God did not make us alike. God did not
make me like Billy Graham. He made me Oscar Thompson. I
cannot help it. I do not want to help it. I am who I am. I must be
me. *If I am not me* in God's economy, then I am *wrong* in my
attitude. I must accept the way I am. When Jesus fills me, I can
accept me. I can be balanced.

I tell my preachers, "Do not go out there and say I wish I
were like . . ." No, you are blaming God if you do not like the
way God made you. God has a ministry, and he has a plan for
you. I do not care how great that other fellow's ministry is. You

be faithful in the things that you can do. You are not to judge yourself by your peer group. You are you. Do not be condemned by anybody else's standards. You are you.

Do not worry about that achievement level either. You achieve for the glory of God. As you achieve, you lay your successes at his feet. Isn't that sweet? Do all that you do to the *glory* of God.

Now, if we can achieve that balance, we will achieve it at the cross. That is why I glory in the cross. That is why Jesus died for me. That is where I can find forgiveness of sin. That is where I do not have to blame anyone else. That is where God's goodness and love flow to me. That is where I find achievement. I do not have to be frustrated, comparing myself with a thousand other people. I am who I am. "Thank you, Father. Now take me and flow through me beyond myself in Circle 1 to my Concentric Circles."

3
Shaking the Family Tree

As we move beyond the Self and Circle 1, we make a survey of Circle 2 and list the Immediate Family. Here I list Carolyn, my wife, and Damaris, my daughter. Because my father has gone to be with the Lord and I am the only son, I also list my mother in Circle 2. I am in constant contact with her. These three are my Immediate Family.

A sample of the survey sheet is provided on pages 167 and 168. A sheet should be kept on each person in your Concentric Circles.

The Immediate Family

Your Immediate Family will be those who live under your roof. If you are away from home and not married, your survey for Circle 2 will include your mother and father. If you are married, your Immediate Family will be your spouse and children. The rest of your family will go under Circle 3, Relatives, which we will discuss later in this chapter.

If you are not the channel of God's love to meet the needs of those in your Immediate Family, forget about Afghanistan. We get concerned about the ends of the earth, yet we cannot meet the needs of our own families.

Love is meeting needs. If I am not allowing God to use me to meet my family's needs, my evangelism becomes hyprocrisy. No wonder we do not want to share the gospel with the whole world. If it is not real at home, it is not going to be real out there.

Now you ask, "What does this have to do with evangelism?"

Everything. God has given the home as the context in which we learn to build relationships.

Let me illustrate. I have many students who come to me and say, "Dr. Thompson, I did not do very well in high school. I did not do very well in college." They come in and weep. They say, "I want to go into the ministry. I want to study Greek and Hebrew, but I did not do very well before. But now, I am going to do my best."

I do everything in my power to help them, to encourage them. But this is the tragedy. Those students have lost a background in the school of knowledge. They have not taken seriously the tools which they were given on which to build the rest of their lives. Education is a discipline. Education is an opportunity to learn how to use your tools. You then use these tools the rest of your life.

The same principle applies to relationships. If you blow the opportunity of learning how to use the tools of relationship that God has given you in the home, then you have blown everything.

What are you going to do? As you move through your Circles, you find a child who is in trouble with the police. He has already been in trouble with himself. He is not free with himself. So he is in trouble with his parents; he is in trouble with his teachers; he is in trouble with Providence. He is in trouble with everyone because he did not learn right relationships in his home. If we do not use the home as the basis for building relationships, we have lost our tools.

Meeting the Family's Needs

Let me tell you how I try to meet my family's needs everyday. First I ask myself, what is my *daily* responsibility to my wife, Carolyn? God has put me into her life, and I accept his conditions for my relationship to her. I am there to meet her needs, whatever those needs are.

Then I have a Damaris. She is fourteen years old. She is

blond, green-eyed, and irrepressible. She just keeps coming.

Damaris has a dog named Neigette, which in French means snowflake. He is white and very "flaky." When the alarm goes off in the morning, I cringe. Damaris opens her bedroom door, and here he comes. Our bedroom is about seventeen feet long. Neigette takes about three steps, flies through the air, and lands on me. I get my morning bath.

I yell for Damaris to get the dog. She replies, "He is just loving you." I do not have that kind of need!

But Damaris has learned a lot from hearing me speak. She has learned the language. I always know if she really has a need because when she really has a need, she sits down and very maturely explains what the need is.

Sometimes she just comes popping through and says, "I have a need," and keeps going. It is like going through and dropping a fifty-cent piece in the proverbial slot machine and pulling the lever. Who knows? Dad might be in the right mood, and she may hit the jackpot. So that is Damaris.

Then there is my dear eighty-two-year-old mother. She loves everything in sight. What a precious soul she is. She has a ministry of writing. I suppose she writes close to one hundred letters a month. She does not just write empty, sentimental little notes. They are sweet, but they also meet needs. They will uplift you and encourage you.

One day I said, "Dear, how do you do it?"

"Well," she replied, "Honey, when I miss Oscar, when I get lonely, when I get afraid, or when I become blue missing Oscar's touch or his voice, I find somebody who has a need. I allow the Lord to reach out to them through me. When I comfort others, God comforts me."

These three are my Immediate Family, my Circle 2. "But," you may say, "your second circle does not have any lost people in it." That's right. But if you are not loving those in your second circle, you are surely not going to love those in your Circle 7 very well. You see, this life-style is loving the saved and the lost.

Now back to Carolyn, whom I list on a survey sheet all by herself. I love Carolyn so when I begin to pray for her, I say, "Father, what are her needs?" *Love is meeting needs.*

One of my friends said, "You know, I really did not know what my wife's needs were until I asked her. One of her needs is to get out of the house occasionally and go shopping. She likes me to go with her, but I do not really like to go. That is one of her needs; so I go anyway."

I understand how my friend feels. I grew up with a mother and two older sisters who loved to go shopping. Since I was the baby brother, I had to go along.

"Be quiet. Stand still. We will be through in a little while," they would say. A little while could mean anywhere from five minutes to six hours. It usually meant the latter.

Well, my wife is just like my mother and two sisters. When we go to the mall, we walk from one end to the other at least six times. We shop at every shop. We look at everything in each shop, and I do believe almost always we go back to that first shop and buy the first thing she saw.

Though I detest shopping, I do it because Carolyn likes me to go along with her. I have learned that whatever her needs are, whatever it costs, that is what I want to do.

A Christian Marriage

In our day and time, the trouble is that we do not understand what Jesus meant when he spoke of love. We usually say, "I love *me* and I want *you* to make *me* happy. If you do not make me happy, then I am going to split."

That is not a Christian marriage. A Christian marriage means I am committing myself first to Jesus Christ and then to my wife. Because my commitment is first to Christ, I accept my wife on his conditions with all the immeasurable love that he has. My attitude toward her is going to be like Jesus' attitude toward the church. He loved it, and he poured out his life for it.

Do not settle for anything less if you are not married. I am lead-pipe serious. That is the relationship I have with my dear, beautiful, glorious, wonderful wife.

I am already trying to teach this principle to my daughter. Damaris came in the other morning, stuck her head into the dressing room. "Daddy, Western days at school today."

"That's great. So?" I answered.

"May I wear your hat?"

My first reaction was, "Of course not!" My hat was a fifty-dollar gift. It is a beautiful, straw hat I enjoy wearing sometimes in the summer. Besides, it was raining that morning. Damaris is just at that age when all the boys would want to knock her hat off. I know! I used to do that myself.

Guess what? She wore the hat! But her mother wrapped it in cellophane. Carolyn knew how to meet Damaris's need and mine. *Love is meeting needs.*

But many people are not learning that at home. Our best school for teaching relationships is not teaching as it should be. We have tried to place the task elsewhere: schools, church, Sunday School, youth organizations, and government. But the home is where we learn to be what we are.

I shared this principle in class one day. Several days later one of my students came to my office and said, "Dr. Thompson, I really blew it."

I said, "Oh! Tell me about it."

He said, "We have just started seminary and my wife has been homesick. This is the first time she has ever lived a long distance from her family. The house we have here is so much less than the one we left. Anyway, yesterday she was just miserable. She said she didn't know what to do. I know God wants us here. I began to lecture her. I said, 'Honey, you know that God has called us here. You know that this is our calling.' "

His lecture was such a blessing to her. She became quiet and whipped. He felt so pious as he went off to study Greek.

That's one reason I tell my students, "Preach to the congregations, not to your wives!"

The next morning in class God captured that student. The man said, "I did not meet that woman's needs." He went back to her and asked, "Honey, forgive me? I am so blind that I do not even know what your needs are."

She said, "I was just lonely, afraid, and insecure in a new city, in a new life. I love you. All I wanted was for you to put your arms around me and hold me and say, 'Baby, it is all right! ' "

Do you see where we are going? Has this ever happened to you? Are there times when you need to take your child in your arms and just listen? Are there times when you need to turn the "box" off and listen to your family? Learn their needs.

Several months ago I was teaching a night session for our seminary students' wives. We were talking about Concentric Circles.

After our second meeting, one of the wives asked to talk with me. She said, "My husband has been discouraged with one of his classes. I work all day long. I arrive at home after a hard day's work and rush to get dinner. Then I walk to our session. He could at least bring me. But after the evening session last week as I got to the door of our house, I had that ringing in my ears, 'Love is meeting needs! Love is meeting needs! ' "

She continued, "The first thing I saw when I walked through the door was my husband sitting in his easy chair watching the football game."

He said, "Honey, will you bathe the kids and put them to bed?"

She said, "There were the dirty dishes from dinner. The house was a wreck. He had done nothing all day long." She sighed and continued, "I took a deep breath. I did not *feel* very loving, but I decided to trust the Lord to love through me. What are his needs? Well, the first is for me not to create a scene."

So she said to her husband, "I have been wanting to see the children all day. This will give me an opportunity."

By the time she had changed clothes and started to get the children, she heard the bath water running. He had already begun to bathe the children.

He said, "If you will towel off this one, I will take care of the other one."

She continued, "You know, God began to do something in my heart toward my husband. There has been so much pressure between us lately. It all seems to be gone. I have come to realize that my own responsibility before God is to be *his* channel for *meeting needs.*"

A Word of Warning. I want to discuss with you something very important about relationships at this point. Husbands and wives, read this very carefully. Underline it! Remember it! When you accept Jesus Christ's conditions for marriage, it means that no other human is to be closer to you than your mate. If you let a close friend or relative be closer than your mate, something is *radically* wrong with your relationship.

That is the reason a child leaves father and mother. Until this point, that was the closest relationship. Marriage changes the parent-child relationship. Sometimes people do not realize this. But it is extremely important in the marriage relationship.

Meeting Children's Needs

Now, what about the children? What about their needs? You see, God has put us in a school—the home. The *subject* is *relationships.* Parents are to meet children's needs. Babies cannot meet their own needs. Parents have to. If you really want to meet that child's needs, you will train that child to love other children and to meet their needs.

Something really thrills me. Damaris, as I said, is fourteen. She is the joy of my life. There is always something new.

She seems to make more money than I do. I kid you not. The other day we were at the restaurant and I said, "Oh, Honey, I am fresh out."

She said, "Daddy, I will take care of it." She whipped out a ten-dollar bill and paid for our lunch. She is a baby-sitter. At our church we have a program where teens are taught to take care of children. The Red Cross, the fire fighters, and police officers all come in and teach them what to do in case of emergencies.

Damaris is a licensed baby-sitter. The kids all over the hill where we live love her. She gets more calls now than I do. She gets calls, puts them down in her little calendar date book; then off she goes to baby-sit. I wait up for her. Sometimes it is 1:00 or 1:30 AM, but I wait up.

Damaris loves the children. I know that my little girl is growing up because she is *learning* to *love*. She is learning to *meet needs*. It is beautiful.

When I pray for Damaris, I relate to my daughter's needs. I ask myself, *Who are the people who will have an influence on her?* Obviously, her teachers. I list all of her teachers on Damaris's survey sheet, and I pray for them. You had better pray for the people who have authority over your children. They *will* influence them.

Listen to Meet Needs. Fathers and mothers, we need to listen to our children. We need to listen to our teens and hear from them what their needs are. Sometimes *what we feel* their needs to be are not really what they are at all. Listen, teens are crying out for love, crying out for mothers and fathers to really know what they are going through and to really know what their needs are.

A seventeen-year-old bounced into my office one day. She seemed to be a little rebel on wheels. But she broke down and cried as she admitted, "If only my parents would tell me one time when to get in at night! Do they really care?"

Parents, we do not need to be Hitlers driving our children from us. We need to be praying for these children whom God has given us. We need to be praying for the Holy Spirit to speak to them, to convict them. But most important, and please do not miss this, we need to be praying for the Holy Spirit to make us the kind of mothers and fathers our children need. We must pray that we will *listen*, that we will *hear*, that we will *meet* their needs. There is no better *success story* in the world than that of a mother and father who can look at their baby who has developed into a man or woman and who radiates the character of Jesus Christ, who knows and cares about the needs of others. Friends, that is success!

I had a student last year who asked us to pray with him about his thirteen-year-old son. He was beginning to be rebellious and had not come to know the Lord. We began to pray. But we also prayed for that daddy to be the kind of father his son needed.

About three months later, the fellow came into class and said, "I have something to say. Last night my son ran into my bedroom in the middle of the night and cried out, 'Daddy, I'm lost.' "

Of course, spiritual dad that he was, he said, "Son, you're not lost; you're right here in the house with Mother and Dad."

His son cried, "No, Daddy, I am lost. I am lost from God! I am lost from the Lord!"

Daddy finally caught on, got up, and shared the gospel. His son trusted the Lord. The boy was not convinced but convicted. That comes about through intercessory prayer.

Finding Your Kissing Kin

Circle 3 is Relatives. That can go on *ad infinitum*. You may say, "I do not know most of my family." Well, shake the family tree. You will be surprised who will fall out. You will find people you never thought of, but you have a relationship with them that is blood kin or marriage kin. That puts them in your line of relationships.

List the names of these relatives. Get as much information about them as you can. Fill out a survey sheet for each. The key is to find their needs. Then all you have to do is show an interest and a love for people. They will turn to you and say, "Oh, you care!" Listen, people, that is living! *Love is meeting needs.*

But you say, "Good grief, I have a zillion relatives! You mean I am suppose to pray for all of them?" You may even think of giving up.

I realize that you cannot pray for each relative every day. But write those names on your survey sheets in your notebook (see pp. 167 and 168) and then during your quiet time flip through your survey sheets, sometimes just looking at names.

Do you remember Susanna Wesley? She was John Wesley's mother. She had nineteen children in twenty-two years. She was very busy. To take care of everyone she had to organize very carefully. Once she was asked which of her children she loved most. She replied, "The one that is hurt at the moment." Do you know why? Because of their needs. *Love is meeting needs.* As you move through your relatives, you will begin to know who has needs at that particular time. It's very important to be close to your family. It sometimes helps you to know yourself.

Pray in Specifics

Do not pray in blanket form. You know, "Lord, bless them all." Too often we come to God and say, "Lord, just bless us." No! God expects us to pray for specific things. Sometimes we do not want to pray specifically because we are afraid that God might not answer specifically. If you do not pray specifically, as we have learned in James 4:2, "you do not have because you do not ask," how will you ever know if God answers prayer unless you pray specifically?

Living Up to a Name

How many of you know what your name means? The Jew in biblical times gave his child a name with a meaning that he expected the child to live up to. But we just say, "Well, sounds good; I will call him." It does not matter. I was interested in what my name meant. Was I suprised! *William* means "to conquer" or "the one who goes forth to conquer." *Oscar* is a fine Swedish name that is usually what you call a pet puppy. It means "bounding forth to war." Now friend, I am a lover, not a fighter. I really was not too pleased with *William Oscar*. So I thought, *Well Thompson just has to improve*. I wrote to the American Genea-logical Society. They sent back my family crest and my family's history.

The family crest has on it three red falcons and a gold-mailed fist with a broken lance. Underneath in French is inscribed: "We wish for a fair fight." Well, sometimes you win and sometimes you don't.

Aunt Alice

Move through your whole family. As you begin to intercede for these loved ones in Circle 3, and later for Friends in Circle 4 and so on through the whole survey, you will need to be sensi-tive to the Holy Spirit's leadership to those who are in the deep-est need.

In time, you are going to find several hundred people in your survey. There will be aunts and uncles and kinsmen you never dreamed were there.

One of my friends was working through Circle 3 and remembered his great aunt Alice. Dick had met Aunt Alice sev-eral times at family reunions, but he was not even sure where she lived. He wrote his mom and said, "Mom, where is Aunt Alice? I have her on my prayer list. Can you get her address for me?"

Dick's mother wrote back and reported that Aunt Alice was eighty-two years old and in a rest home about eighty-five miles from where Dick lived. She sent him Aunt Alice's address. Then on Aunt Alice's birthday, Dick sent her a birthday card.

Aunt Alice wrote back, thrilled to hear from him. In several weeks, Dick called her to set up a time when he and his wife could drive out to visit her.

Dick introduced his wife to his aunt Alice, and they talked about the pleasantries of the day. Then Aunt Alice asked, "Well, Honey, tell me what you do?"

"I am in Southwestern Seminary studying for the ministry," Dick answered.

Then Aunt Alice asked, "Well, what do you study?"

Dick replied, "Basically, I study that the most important word in the English language, apart from proper nouns, is *relationship*. Like the relationship we now have. I also study that if you really love someone, you meet his needs."

"Oh, that really sounds interesting; tell me more," Aunt Alice said.

"Well," Dick replied, "the basic need in the life of every individual is to know Jesus Christ in a very personal and intimate way."

"That sounds very interesting," she said. "Please tell me what you mean?"

He then shared with her the gospel: how a person comes to know the Lord, how to have sins forgiven, and how to live in a right relationship with the Father and with those about him.

Aunt Alice looked at Dick, big tears filling her eyes, and whispered, "Son, I have been a member of a church for years, but I have never done that. Could I trust Jesus?"

Dick said that he and his wife knelt down beside that dear little lady, and she invited Jesus into her heart. Then months later when I saw Dick, he came up and put his arms around me. He could not talk at first, was kind of choked up. But he hugged me and said, "Doc, this weekend Aunt Alice went to be with the Lord."

Then he added, "Dr. Thompson, what if I had not listed her in my Concentric Circles? What if I had not done my survey?"

I do not want to lay a heavy burden on you, dear friend, because God wants you to take one day at a time. So redeem the time. Use it. You cannot win all of your family in one day. You have the rest of your life, however long that may be, to work through your Concentric Circles. But be available to God. Allow God to love through you to meet people's needs. Live under God's grace and strength. Remember Colossians 2:6. As you received Christ by faith, walk with him by faith.

4

Your Judea, Your Samaria, and Your World

Now you say, "Father, I *cannot* meet the needs of the whole world, but I *can* meet needs in my own world." Do you hear me? "I can love my world. I can meet needs in my Jerusalem. And then, Lord, you may have to drop some bombs in my own life, but you will push me out into Samaria and the uttermost parts of my world."

You cannot give out of your own resources—they are not sufficient. You give out of Jesus' resources. God plus you equals enough *always*.

Reaching Your World

Friends, we can devise many different plans to win the world to Jesus, and that is as it should be. That is how it had better be. But I am not talking about *global* evangelism; I am talking about *your* evangelism. I feel that it is the plan of the Father for us to have a specific strategy to reach *our* world, and say, "This is my world, Father, and I am going to take it!" Then the Spirit of God will fall on us and fill us and speak to us, by us, and through us. "Lord, as long as you leave me in this clay house, I will take my world."

Why a Survey?

You may ask, "Why is a survey necessary?" (Refer to pp. 167 and 168.) For the simple reason that you cannot remember everything you need to remember without writing it on paper.

You need a structure for your evangelism. Nothing ever becomes dynamic until it becomes specific. As you take your survey, you become conscious of people that you never would have thought of. They are in your circle—perhaps in no one else's.

A black pastor friend of mine presented Concentric Circles to his church. The people began to make their surveys and to pray. In one month, the church had sixty professions of faith.

One of my Youth directors told me that his teenagers kept saying, "We know a few kids at school, but we really do not know many people who do not know the Lord." He shared the principles of Concentric Circles with forty of these young people on a retreat. Then he gave them six sheets of paper each and two hours alone to pray and make their surveys. They came back with nineteen hundred names. Several have already been won to the Lord.

So, do a survey. It is important. It is the structure upon which you build.

Remember, as you do your survey, your life-style is *not only* loving the lost but also the saved. Your Concentric Circles will contain many people who are already saved. Do you pray for them? I hope so! They have needs too. They have hurts. Meeting their needs becomes a part of your life-style.

So far, we have moved through three of the seven Concentric Circles, and now we move to the fourth.

Circle 4. In Circle 4 are our Close Friends. Sometimes close friends are closer than relatives. This happens. Close friends have needs too. Do not forget to meet them.

Circle 5. Circle 5 includes Neighbors, Business Associates, and School Friends. Remember, it is so important to write down the information about them on your survey sheet. Why do you want to do this? Because you care. You find out about people that you care about, don't you? Let me illustrate.

Someone asked how I met my wife, Carolyn. I answered that I was pastor of First Baptist Church in Seguin, Texas. I was unmarried, "unseminaried," and "un-everything" else. I was twenty-seven years old. I had gone all the way through Baylor but had not found a wife.

A dear friend, a Methodist layman who loved God, called one day and asked me to come by his office. He wanted to talk to me about visiting a family with a Baptist background.

Passing through his outer office the next day, I met his private secretary. Guess who? Carolyn. There she sat as I stumbled over the chair and the wastepaper basket and knocked the phone off the desk just getting from one door to the next.

When I finally made it to my friend's office, he handed me a sheet of paper with the family's name on it. "But wait," I said, "we will discuss that family later. *Who is that* beautiful creature?" I spent the next three weeks conducting an investigation like the FBI. I wanted to know everything I could about that girl. Then I planned my strategy.

Listen friend, when you care, and God wants to care through you, you will want to know about people. So make your survey.

Getting to Know Your Neighbors

In the city it has become an increasingly greater problem to know our neighbors. But if *love is meeting needs,* and if we want to meet their needs, we must know our neighbors.

My neighbors will not believe that I want to be in heaven with them if I do not want them in my home for dinner or if I do not say hello when we are in our front yards together. We have to know our neighbors before we can meet their needs.

A friend of mine lives across the street from a Korean couple. They are very quiet, and developing a relationship with them has been difficult.

My friend said that after months of trying to build a relationship, there was a death in the couple's family. The wife's mother died. My friend and his wife took the Korean couple a meal.

They took care of their animals and mowed their yard. When the couple came home, they said to my friend, "You have been so kind. We would like to be your friends." Now these friends are ready to listen to the gospel from someone who has shown them love. *Love is meeting needs wherever we are.*

Taking Your World

However, I want to remind you that if you are going to take your world for Jesus, you must have a new and fresh, uncluttered love for our Lord. You and I must be more "self-forgetful." Several years ago when I was so near death, I learned something from the Lord that I will never forget. I learned that it is not how *long* I live; it is *how* I live. Methuselah lived 969 years. So what? Enoch lived 365 years, and the Lord took him. Who would you rather be?

Circle 6

Moving from Neighbors into the sixth circle, you ask, "Who is an Acquaintance?" Well, have you ever been in a grocery store or a restaurant? Do you remember seeing those little name tags worn by the checker or the waitress? Those are not there just for decoration. They bear the names of people who are your acquaintances. We know their faces, and as a Christian, we really need to be sensitive to their names as well. So Circle 6 contains those people that we know casually.

"Hey, You." When you call a waitress, do not say, "Hey, you." One of the deepest needs of any individual is for recognition, and the way to give recognition to a person is to call him by name. It means something to him. It means that you value him and that you are concerned enough to remember his name. Remembering a name may not seem like much, but it means you care.

You meet a need every time you say a person's name. Isn't

that right? Back in the Garden, when God was looking for Adam and Eve, he did not say, "Hey, you!" He said, "Adam, where are you?"

You may say, "I am not good at names." Let me be a little harsh with you. If you do not remember names, it is because you do not care enough. Remembering names takes time. You really have to work at it.

As you begin to work through your Concentric Circles and it becomes a life-style, you will begin to realize how important names are. When you call acquaintances by name, they will never forget you.

I know some preachers who cannot preach their way out of a brown paper sack. They are like dump trucks, but they cannot dump. They are loaded with knowledge and information. Some of them are overloaded. They just do not know how to share it. But let me tell you something. They know how to love, to meet needs; and God uses them. People love them. Why? Because it is difficult not to love someone who loves you.

Remember the Children. Now what about children? Is remembering their names important? Yes! It lets them know you care. There is the story of the little boy who, hearing his father pray the Lord's Prayer, misunderstood the words.

When the little guy repeated the prayer, he said, "Our Father who is in heaven. How did you know my name?"

So in your survey, list your Acquaintances in Circle 6. Get as much information about them as is possible over a period of time. Then as you build that relationship, you will learn their needs.

Circle 7

Finally we come to Circle 7, containing Person X. "Ah," you say, "you have talked about everybody else, but you have not talked about that lost world out there."

Friend, that lost world out there is all we have been talking about. Why? Because somewhere out there in somebody's circle, your Person X may be listed. You see, your Person X may be in my Circle 3. My Person X may be in your Circle 2. To me, some of you are Person X's.

What did Jesus mean in Acts 1:8 when he said "you shall be My witnesses both in Jerusalem, and in all Judea and Samaria, and even to the remotest part of the earth." Just what was he saying to me and to you? Well, to the apostles, their world was first Jerusalem, then Judea and Samaria, and finally the remotest parts of the earth. They started where they were and moved out.

To us he is saying go to *our* Jerusalems, *our* Judeas and Samarias, and outwardly expand. The point he was making is to start where we are.

My world is not your world, and your world is not my world. But if we all put our worlds together, we can take the whole world. Do you know what I have discovered? When God is filling me with his Spirit, he has ways of drawing people into my circles.

Taking Your Temperature

Some of my students say, "I never see anybody who is lost." But I tell them, "You had better check your *spiritual* thermometer." I have found that God has a way of drawing people into my circles when I am walking with him. They just materialize, and I see them.

A "Holy Magnetism"

If you love everyone in your circles, you will find there is a "holy magnetism" through your life. God will draw people *through* you *to* him. Remember, *love is meeting needs.*

Also, let us remind ourselves that when we think of evangelism, we must not think only of Person X. We must think of our whole world, of all our Concentric Circles.

One day, a student sailed into class after we had discussed Concentric Circles.

"Dr. Thompson!" he exploded.

"What's the matter?" I answered.

"Guess what! I just met someone out here who is a Person X. She is a blond and she is beautiful!"

I asked, "And?"

"I want to bring her into my Circle 2."

"She may not want to come," I said, "but I will pray for you."

Remember that God will bring people into your Circle 7, and they may then pass through like a comet, to be there only for a moment; but God puts them there for a purpose. You may never see them again. John 7:38 assures that "from his innermost being shall flow rivers of living water." So if I am walking in the Lord and in agreement with him, I am living.

God says, "Here is one of my children. I can bear fruit in his life." So God draws someone into the life of his child knowing that he will meet the needs of Person X. When Person X is touched by a child of God, that person receives power.

Remember when Jesus was walking through the crowds one day? They were jostling him on every side, shoving and pushing and eager to press in upon him. Suddenly Jesus turned and asked, "Who touched my garments?" (Mark 5:25-34). His disciples could not understand and asked Jesus what he meant since many people were touching him. But Jesus answered that somebody had really touched him and he had felt power leave him. Then a little woman standing nearby confessed that she had touched him. Through his power, she was healed.

Person X Needs You

Dear friend, someone is going to "touch" you. Maybe it will be someone on an airplane as we discussed in chapter 1, someone with a need. It may be on a train or a bus. But when someone touches you, do they touch God's power? And will you take the time to meet the needs of that Person X?

Do you understand what I am saying? People will pass into and out of your life. You may never know when. But be ready.

Pray, "Father, here I am." He knows who needs loving and will put that unknown person into your Circle 7. Sometimes God brings a person into your life in an irritating circumstance, but he may be testing your response to his grace.

Some of my students who formerly had not been able to find lost people will admit, "You know, when I am walking in submission to my Lord, I bump into more people accidentally who need Jesus than I ever could run down on purpose." This is God bearing fruit in their lives as they become aware of and meet the needs of Person X.

Don't Exclude to Include

So we see that we must remember to include Person X who, like a comet, comes into our lives only for a moment and then passes through. We may never see him again, not in this lifetime. He may touch us only for a moment. Will he touch power?

Do you know what I have realized? The person who has right relationships has the power of the Holy Spirit not only *resident* within his life but also moving through his life as well. The Holy Spirit is always resident in a Christian; but when he is allowed to be free, he is constantly moving in and through your life to meet needs. You may call it the fullness of the Spirit, call it the great unction of God that is upon your life, call it whatever. Just remember that the Holy Spirit will engineer circumstances to bring Person X into your life knowing that you will be faithful to love him and to meet his needs.

A "Good-Buddy Story"

One night, driving from Houston, Carolyn, Damaris, and I were listening to the CB radio. If you have one, do not be afraid of it. If you know only ten or twelve words, you can use a CB. I enjoy talking on it and never know whom I will meet.

My handle is not Sky Pilot or the Preacher. With those names, some people would not talk to me. So mine is Jelly

Bean. With that handle, I talk to everybody.

It was late that night, driving from Houston, and I was tired. I was talking on the CB to help keep myself awake. Damaris had settled down on the back seat. We had cleared the city, and the chatter had died down. No one else was saying much so I started talking to a fellow called Rocky Mountain.

I asked him, "What is your home 20?"

He answered.

"Where are you going?"

He replied, "San Antonio."

We talked on a little more. Then everything grew silent for awhile.

After awhile Rocky Mountain said, "Jelly Bean, I am going to San Antonio to see a preacher. If that preacher cannot help me, I am going straight to hell!"

Damaris, who was almost asleep in the backseat, came over the seat and said, "What did he say?"

I said, "Friend, I know that you are going to find this hard to believe, but Jelly Bean is a preacher."

He said, "Jelly Bean, a preacher!"

I answered, "That's right, and I would be happy to talk with you."

To make a long story short, at the next easy-on, easy-off service station, I pulled off and climbed into the car with him. In fifteen or twenty minutes, he invited Christ into his life.

You never know. You just never know where they are. The Holy Spirit just draws them. They are there. They are hungry. They are hurting, but they sense the world does not care.

You see, I will never see Rocky Mountain on earth again. He came into my life, and he passed out like a comet. And there are Person X's whom you will never see again. But God holds *you* responsible.

You have a Jerusalem. You have a Judea. You have a Samaria. And you have an uttermost part of the earth. Someday the Lord is going to ask, "What did you do with it?"

5
The Greatest Step—Intercession

The one indispensable ingredient in a great church, the one indispensable ingredient in a close walk with God is knowing how to pray.

But real prayer is more than "cliché praying": asking God to bless the meal or praying before a Sunday School class or pulling the alarm of prayer in a time of trouble.

When I was a little boy, my family would go into San Antonio for the day from our home in Gonzales. The only time we went to San Antonio was when my daddy was going to sell cattle. I had to stay with my mother and two sisters.

I learned from those early experiences that shopping with women is not easy. They wanted to look at everything on God's green earth. It was terrible, especially for a four- or five-year-old boy.

Finally, after the ladies had finished their shopping, we would wait for my dad at our meeting place in the lobby of the Gunter Hotel. I would be tired and fretful after all that shopping, but I did not want to sit and wait. So my sisters, Laurel and Nelwyn, would take me for walks. While we walked, I had questions about everything.

One day on one of these walks, I saw a big red box on a pole with a glass window in front.

"What's that?" I asked.

"That's a fire alarm," Nelwyn answered.

I saw the little hammer hanging by the box. I listened as my sister explained to me that if there were a fire emergency, someone would take the hammer, break the glass, pull the fire alarm, and then the fire fighters would come. The idea really fascinated me. Remembering this incident caused me later to make a comparison. Red letters beneath the box read KNOCK OUT GLASS *ONLY* IN CASE OF EMERGENCY. Many people have a prayer box which they use much like the fire alarm. Only in case of an emergency do they really get earnest about intercession.

I have heard that preventive medicine is better than dealing with a disease after you get it. We could prevent much tragedy in our hearts and lives—as well as in the hearts and lives of our children, our churches, our Concentric Circles—if we continually prayed for each other before tragedy starts.

Often we wait until our child stumbles and gets into trouble or becomes a problem or we wait until someone gets desperately ill or we see a marriage going on the rocks. At times we need to pray like this; but wouldn't praying constantly, like Paul did, be much better? We need continually to pray through our Concentric Circles.

Your Love May Abound

Paul showed us how to intercede. He said, "This I pray, that your love may abound still more and more in real knowledge and all discernment" (Phil. 1:9). Paul was praying for the Philippians to have wisdom and insight to meet people's needs. Have you ever prayed Philippians 1:9 for anyone? Have you ever prayed for God's wisdom in you to meet another person's needs?

If You Lack Wisdom

When you pray, pray for wisdom. You may ask, "Holy Father, give me wisdom to deal with this person." God *will* give it. When you pray for wisdom, do not sit around waiting *to feel wise.* Begin to move. As you are going, God will supply the wisdom. "If any of you lacks wisdom, let him ask of God, who gives to all men generously" (Jas. 1:5).

Sometimes we parents say, "I want to love my children. I

want to meet their needs." But sometimes we unwisely get *wants* and *needs* confused. If we meet all their *wants*, we hurt them. There is a difference between meeting wants and needs. We are like the little girl who found her kitten out in the rain. Because she loved it so much, she did not want it to catch cold. So what did she do? She stuck it in the oven and turned up the heat! We do not doubt her sincerity, but what about her wisdom?

Praying for Wisdom

My Damaris is in high school now. She is becoming beautiful. I pray for Damaris's wisdom. She has many temptations now. She is making many decisions. As the father of an only child, I am trying to hold her but yet to shove her at the same time. If I hold her too tightly, she will never grow.

I do not know how long I will be in this clay house. None of us know. We need to pray now that our children will have wisdom. We need to pray now that we will have wisdom to instruct them.

I must pray that Damaris will be sensitive to the leading of the Holy Spirit. So I pray, "Father, give Damaris wisdom to make the decisions she needs to make today." Do you know what I have found? I do not fuss at her when I am praying for her. When I pray for her, I find that my temper is not as sharp and that I am not as frustrated with her when she does dumb things, just as I have done dumb things. I find that when I pray for Damaris, I see her come through with a blaze of wisdom.

I pray, too, for that boy she may marry some day. I pray for him now. I pray for him daily that God will prepare him to be the right kind of man. I pray that God is teaching him wisdom as he grows and matures.

Now, you may think that I have fallen off the lowest limb of a tree and hit my head; but if I have, just leave me in my befuddled state. I like it because I can sense what God is doing, and I can see my prayers becoming reality. God is moving. He is directing and leading.

Remember, though, that before we can pray effectively for

others, *we* have to be right with the Lord. We have to take Self (Circle 1) before the Lord and clear out the sin in that circle; then we can get down to business on Circles 2 through 7.

Are there ruptured relationships in your life? Matthew 5:23-24 says that even if *your brother* is upset *with you,* go to him and *you* be the reconciler. Because *you* are the one who is living in victory, *you* are to be the *reconciler.*

So keep your conscience clear. If the Holy Spirit brings something to your mind that is wrong in your life, set it straight. Deal with it. Keep short accounts with God. What we need is a personal revival, a personal walk, letting the Lord work out his redemptive purpose in and through our lives. Sometimes I meet people who have difficulty with Concentric Cirlces because they do not want to right relationships in those circles. But it is impossible to be right with God and wrong with those around us.

But remember that God holds us accountable for everyone who comes into our Concentric Circles. He wants us to love people and intercede for them. Remember that *love is meeting needs.*

Reaching Our Family

Some students have great difficulty working through Circle 2 and Circle 3, their families. They say they do not want to pray for Mom and Dad because of bitterness between them, perhaps even over coming to the seminary. There are ruptured relationships. Many students want to come to the seminary and go directly to Circle 7, maybe to Rhodesia or somewhere else around the world to share the Word of Jesus. But they do not want to pray for any or some of those people in their inner circles.

We have ruptured relationships; but God says that when Jesus becomes Lord of our lives, we must surrender forever the right to choose whom we will love.

I told a class where I shared Concentric Circles, "Now you are responsible for building bridges, interceding for your family, and making sure that you meet their needs." If you are going to bear the character of Jesus Christ, you are going to have to love, and *love is meeting needs.*

One of the students, Jim, came in one day after we had discussed Concentric Circles and said, "Dr. Thompson, my dad is a nominal Christian; but when he learned that I was going into the ministry, he became furious. He told me that he did not mind my being a Christian, but he did not want me to become a 'religious nut.' "

Jim's father drove a truck for one of the big truck lines, owned his own rig, and wanted his son to follow in his footsteps. It was somewhat of a tradition. But instead, Jim came to the seminary. As a result, Jim's relationship with his parents was ruptured.

"We had been very close until this happened," Jim explained. "Since then I have just ignored them, as they have ignored me. It has been a hurt to me, but I am going to serve Jesus. My family can do whatever they please."

I asked, "Jim, do you really think you can be right with God and have ruptured relationships with your parents? You need to meet their needs. You need to love them."

Jim answered, "Well, that's right; but I don't know what to do."

So I suggested, "Get the bitterness straight in your own heart and then start to intercede for them, Jim. Right those ruptured relationships."

Jim began to pray for his dad and mom. That same day he came to class brokenhearted and said, "Friends, just please pray for me." Then Jim prayed, "Father, I do not even know if my daddy knows you. But, Father, I have been wrong in my attitude toward my parents. Forgive me of my attitude, and help me meet my parents' needs."

Jim wrote a letter to his parents, asking them to forgive him because of his bitterness and the broken relationship. He told them that he loved them.

The next day, before the letter had time to reach his parents, Jim received a telephone call from his dad in Dallas. Jim's dad had never before had a route to Dallas, but he said, "Son, I have a route to Dallas this week, and I want to see you."

"Oh, Dad, that's great!"

On that Saturday afternoon, a big rig pulled up in front of Jim's dorm. When Jim opened the dorm door, his tall father stood with tears trickling down his cheeks. "Jim, I am wrong with God," he said. "Can you help me?"

Friend, your world needs you. People all through your Concentric Circles need you. Be a channel of God's love. There is no greater thrill in life than letting the Lord love through you and meet needs through you. That IS the Christian life.

I can tell you hundreds of stories about students with ruptured relationships with their parents who have led those parents to the Lord. Now they have a liberty and a freedom because the ruptures are cleared.

How Do I Intercede?

Do you want to intercede for others? Then pray: "Lord, make me a *channel* of love, give me *wisdom,* and then, Father, *you engineer* circumstances in their lives to *draw* them to you. Be in me *boldness* to *confront* them with *your* love and with *your* message of forgiveness." That is the way you intercede.

Then as you intercede, you pray, "Lord, make me available." Now you do loving things. Let me tell you something. Some people may not respond in love to you. Do not expect everybody to love you back immediately. Sometimes people do not know what to do with your love because many people in your world have never really been loved. Consequently, when you do something loving toward them and meet their needs, they may wonder, "What does he want?"

Do you remember my puppy, Neigette? He is going to love you in spite of everything. So, like Neigette, just keep loving. Be genuine, and do not expect too much too quickly. Make yourself available to God as he leads. After awhile, others will learn that you really care. Meet their needs, and ask God for wisdom as you work with them.

Now that you have done your survey and you are interceding, you and the Lord must work out how you intend to divide your circles to pray for the people. One suggestion is that there are seven days in a week, and you have seven circles. Perhaps you want to take a circle a day or perhaps a long and short circle each day. It does not matter as long as you have a plan. As you pray, ask the Lord to reveal to you the needs of those in your circles. *He* is more interested in your prayer time than even you are.

As we intercede and ask for wisdom, we also ask God to engineer circumstances to draw people to him. Sometimes it gets cloudy and dark when we start doing this. Sometimes crisis comes, but do not let that alarm you. Sometimes darkness comes before light. Sometimes it is a desert for months. But keep loving as you pray.

The Story of John

There came to our church a lady by the name of Alice. Her husband's name was John. Because the ladies in Sunday School built bridges and reached out to Alice, she came to know the Lord.

Then Alice became concerned about her husband and said to me, "Please pray for John. He has never been in a Protestant service in his life."

Well, in a few weeks John came quite reluctantly to his first Protestant service. It scared him to death. Do you know why? He was under conviction. He did not know what was going on. He had heard the gospel and realized that something was missing in his life.

Six fellows in our church manned our SWAT (Spiritual Weapons and Tactics) team. "The weapons of our warfare are not of the flesh, but divinely powerful for the destruction of fortresses" (2 Cor. 10:4). These men knew how to intercede; they knew how to build bridges to people.

I gave them John's name, and they descended with gusto. They began to intercede for him; they began to love him. They took him to lunch and played tennis with him. They knew he needed Christian fellowship.

One day he came home and laughingly told Alice, "Honey, those Baptists are after me." Well, he liked the attention, but it also frightened him because he was under conviction of sin.

Each of these men, though, came back to say, "Pastor, I do not understand. I have tried to confront John with the very essentials of the gospel, but I am having difficulty."

I only said, "Keep praying. God has something in mind." You know, intercessory prayer is like a guided missile. It always hits its target. Here was our prayer for John. "Father, you engineer circumstances in John's life to *draw* him to yourself."

John continued to come to the services every Sunday, and we continued to pray. This went on for a couple of months.

By this time John had come to love the fellowship of our people but was so under conviction that he was miserable. So what did he do? He joined the National Guard. Doing that, he would miss services two Sundays a month.

John's decision was quite a shock to Alice, and she was so discouraged. I said, "Alice, you just pray that you will be the kind of wife that John needs and love him. That is your responsibility. Do not try to be the Holy Spirit. God knows what he is about."

Often when we begin to pray, circumstances do not go the way we would have planned them. Sometimes they really get tough. But do not let that alarm you. Who is bigger, *God* or the *problem?* You see, the Lord knew John better than we did. Through all of these circumstances God was working.

One day, when everything had seemed to go badly for John, he walked across a rental yard talking to a fellow about renting a truck. John turned the air blue with profanity as he complained to the fellow about everything.

"John," this other fellow said, "I want to tell you something. I used to be under pressure like you are until I gave my life to Jesus Christ."

John hushed. He got into the truck and drove away. The fellow had not confronted him with the gospel; he had just gently shared.

The next day was Sunday and guard day. John was relieved that he did not have to go to church. Walking across the parade grounds talking to one of the other sergeants, again he complained about everything.

All of a sudden, this other fellow said, "John, you know I used to feel that way. I was in such a turmoil until I gave my life to Christ."

John thought, *Good grief!* He was a photographer for the guard. He went into the darkroom, closed the door, kind of sighed, and said, "Oh, it is good to get out of that bright sunshine and into this darkness."

But there, working under the enlarger, was a guy who

quipped, "Well, you know what the Scriptures say, John, 'men loved the darkness rather than light; for their deeds were evil' " (John 3:19).

POW! There is power in prayer. There is *no human way* this whole scene could have been arranged. The whole plan came from a living, loving God. What was happening? A sovereign God was *answering* prayer and *engineering* circumstances to draw a *life* to *himself*. That is the work of the Holy Spirit.

John went home and said to Alice, "Honey, it is not just those Baptists. Christians are everywhere!"

The life of the apostle Paul was saturated with prayer. If you read carefully the life of our Lord Jesus, you will understand that his life was permeated with prayer. And if we think we are going to make it without praying, we are badly mistaken. No wonder people are not converted and lives are not changed.

If you do not believe in a supernatural God, you will be in trouble because you will think, *I am going to have to manipulate this whole thing!* You try, but you may get your hands burned.

Believing in a supernatural God does not mean that you become passive and do not do anything. No, you are moving; but while you move, remember that you are God's instrument. The direction comes from him. Your job is to intercede, to pray for people, and to meet needs.

Not to keep you in suspense any longer about John, the next week he came charging past the receptionist, past my secretary, and into my office. Closing the door to my office, he announced, "Preacher, I am in trouble!"

"What's the matter?" I asked.

"I am going to get a divorce!"

"You are going to do what?"

"I am going to get a divorce!" he repeated.

"Why in the world would you want to do that?" I asked him. "You love that woman!"

He said, "I cannot give spiritual leadership to my home."

And I said, "Brother, I have heard many reasons for divorce, but this is not one of them." This was a weird conversation, but this is just the way it went.

"I know what you are going to say," John grumbled. "I know that you are going to say that I need to trust Jesus."

"You said that," I told him.

"But that is what you are going to tell me," he repeated as he turned and walked out of my office.

I started to follow him, but the Holy Spirit said, "No, everything is under control. It will be all right."

John got back into his truck and headed toward Dallas. Somewhere on the turnpike between Fort Worth and Dallas, he stopped his truck, got out, knelt down pretending to change a tire, and said, "Lord Jesus, save me."

Later that afternoon John came back to my office. "Signals check," he said and smiled. "Everything is all right. Now I *can* be the spiritual leader in my home." And off he went.

The Holy Spirit had convicted John of his condition before God. You see, you can *convince;* but it takes the Holy Spirit of God to *convict.* My convincing someone only makes him feel guilty; but when a person is convicted, he can see that he is held in high treason against heaven's King.

Let me share with you something else. Some people are very difficult. You think they are impossible. They will not come to church, and you think, *If I cannot get them to church, how in the world can they be saved?*

The truth is that they *can* be saved as well outside the church as inside it. First-century Christians were saved without a church building. Erroneously we think sometimes that the only place someone can be saved is inside the church building.

God Specializes in the Impossible

Another example of how God wants to draw people to him and heal broken relationships is illustrated by a student named Jeff whose brother had left home in the late sixties with the hippy movement. His family had not seen him since.

Jeff told me about his brother, saying, "He has broken my parents' hearts. We do not know if he is dead or alive. I am not sure I want to know what has happened to him. Can I leave him out of my Circle 2?"

"No, Jeff," I answered, "God put your brother in your circle for a reason. Write his name down in your survey. Intercede for him. Get your attitude right toward him."

As Jeff met God's conditions of relationship toward his brother, he received a deep burden to pray for him. Months passed and nothing happened. But Jeff was faithful and continued to pray. Then all of a sudden there came this inexplicable, unexplainable circumstance that drew this brother to Fort Worth. He called Jeff. Jeff called me at 2:30 AM after he had talked with his brother.

"Dr. Thompson, are you awake?"

"Well, I am now," I laughed.

Jeff then explained, "Dr. Thompson, this is Jeff. My brother just called. I have been praying and here he is. He is coming to class with me in the morning."

"Good," I said, "tomorrow I will teach the class how to come to know Jesus in a personal way." And I did! And he did! Jeff's brother accepted the Lord in my office after class.

I want to tell you something. When *you* get things right in your own life with God, he will begin to engineer impossible circumstances to bring more people into your Concentric Circles to have their needs met than you could ever run down on purpose. You become fulfilled.

And Still Another

I had another student come to me and say, "Dr. Thompson, when my brother got into the drug culture two years ago, things really got bad at home; so he left. He wanted to do his own thing. He was addicted, probably selling it, and everything else. What should I do? I love him, but I feel so helpless. I do not know how to find him."

"Well, that is no problem," I told him. "God knows where your brother is."

Sometimes we pray like, "Father, I do not know if you can do this or not." But when you intercede for someone, it is like a guided missile. It is instantaneous. And it is on target. There is no defense.

That student began praying for his brother. One day the student came into my office and said, "I received a call from my brother. He has been converted and is going home."

My student almost sounded disappointed because he did not get to witness to his brother. But let me say this. He was ready to witness to him; his heart was right with God; and through his intercession, his brother was freed to choose the Lord.

I was told one day, "My brother will not get within a hundred yards of a church. We cannot reach him. You try to talk to him. . . ." "Dear friend," I said, "you can pray for him. He cannot resist prayer because God breaks down those walls and barriers. You pray, 'Father, open his eyes to his spiritual condition and set him free. Lord, engineer circumstances in his life to draw him to you.' It will thrill you to see what God will do if you make your life available."

We have a sensational God. He deals in the impossible. He specializes in the impossible.

You must intercede for those in your circles. You must pray for God to meet their spiritual, physical, or whatever needs they have. You are his vessel. You must be available.

Another student who had graduated was back on campus several months ago. Entering my office, he laid his ragged Concentric Circle notebook in my hands.

"Dr. Thompson, here is my notebook," he said. "I want you to look at it."

That young man—who had never led anyone to the Lord before—in one year, had led to the Lord thirty-eight people listed in his Concentric Circles.

Senior Adults, We Need You

We need to mobilize our retired people, shut-ins, and our senior adults in our churches to pray. Because they have more time to pray, they can provide a powerful ministry in our churches.

Over the years, I have had shut-ins and retired people pray for me. How thankful I am for them. While I was at Baylor, a dear little saint prayed for me. At the time I had a church in Gonzales, and I drove back to Baylor late every Sunday night.

"My husband has already gone to be with the Lord," this dear lady explained to me. "I am here alone and have much time to pray. I am going to pray for you each Sunday night until I know that you are back in the dorm."

One night just out of Round Rock, north of Austin, I came upon a terrible wreck. I was the first person on the scene and offered to help. I was delayed several hours. So I did not get in the dorm until about 4:30 AM.

The next weekend I went home to my church. The dear lady who promised to pray for me called, asking, "Where were you Sunday night?"

"What do you mean?" I asked her.

"You kept me awake until 4:30 AM praying for you," she answered. God would not let her go to sleep until I was safe.

Those of you who are up in years, listen to me. You say, "There is not much I can do any more." But do not tell me that because it is not true. You can provide, until Jesus calls you home, the most profitable time of all your life in intercessory prayer. Why not link yourself with some young families who are having problems—do not interfere—just pray for them. Become their "prayer umbrella." Find out about some of the young people who need prayer—all of them need prayer. You can become a vital part of their lives by praying for them.

Also pray daily for your pastor, your church, and the other staff members. Pray for our president, our country. Listen, there are battles to be won in prayer. Become intercessors. That is what we need. Oh, how we need you. Just go through your Concentric Circles and pray for your Jerusalem, your Judea, your Samaria, and your world. It will change your life as much as it changes the many lives you are praying for. Meeting their needs will allow God to meet yours.

It Works in Sunday School Too

Can you imagine what would happen if your Sunday School used Concentric Circles as its outreach program? First, each person would do a survey, then he would begin to intercede every day. Intercession is not a, "Dear Lord, bless me and my wife, my son John and his wife, us four, no more," and jump into bed. No, each person would genuinely intercede by surrounding others with prayer. Intercession would become a lifestyle. Ruptured relationships would be righted. Walls would have to be torn out and new educational buildings built to hold everybody!

Burden from the Lord

Carolyn accepted an adult ladies class at the church I was pastoring. This class had just never made it. With about twenty-five on the class roll, its average attendance was three—two plus the teacher.

The Lord gave Carolyn a heavy burden for this class. She knew that he wanted her to take it. One afternoon she brought home the class roll. Of the twenty-five names on the roll, she knew only five. Carolyn decided that what these ladies needed most at this time was intercession. So an hour or so each day that week she prayed for all twenty-five members. Then she invited to our home the four members who attended occasionally.

A Definite Plan

Carolyn laid out to the four members this plan: Each person, including Carolyn, would take the names of five women who were on the class roll and pray for each one daily. The ladies agreed. They were not to contact the other women, just to pray for them. Now they had a plan. Nothing becomes dynamic until it becomes specific.

Since we had only been at the church a couple of weeks, Carolyn asked if the women knew the others on the roll. Some they knew, but some they didn't.

All four ladies seemed to be familiar with Nancy, who was on Carolyn's prayer list. All four ladies warned, "Do not try to visit Nancy. She and her husband, Harry, are very bitter toward the church. Harry will slam the door in your face. He may even be dangerous to someone from the church. They have been hurt and are very bitter."

Carolyn thanked the ladies for their advice but reminded them that the Lord specializes in cases like this one and that he loves this family. She said, "We will pray that the Lord will engineer circumstances so that we can love them and meet their needs."

About three weeks later an aide from the hospital who attended Carolyn's class called Carolyn saying that Nancy was in the hospital with pneumonia. Carolyn and one of the class members went to visit Nancy. They took her some flowers.

Nancy was appreciative. The class member with Carolyn offered to take care of Nancy's children while she was in the hospital. Nancy really appreciated this help because she did not know how they were going to manage. Finally Carolyn and the other woman left their phone numbers in case there was anything else they could do.

The next day Nancy called Carolyn to say that her husband had been brought to the hospital. He had fallen and injured himself. Immediately Carolyn and I went to the hospital to meet Harry. When we walked into his hospital room, he beamed with appreciation for the ladies' help. Instead of an angry, bitter man, he was just like a big, old teddy bear.

Little Things Mean So Much

The next week when Nancy and Harry went home from the hospital, the Sunday School class took food to them. Nobody threw the women out this time. Nancy and Harry were so grateful. You see, all they needed was God's love to flow through God's people to them. It is difficult to fight genuine love.

God did not cause the sickness or the injury. That is not how he operates. But he allowed it to happen so that Nancy and Harry could see the love of God. He had prepared their hearts to accept us.

Nancy and Harry and their two children were in Sunday School and in church the next Sunday and very rarely missed anything at the church from that time on. God answers prayer. Do we care enough to intercede?

After the experience with Nancy and Harry and after the four ladies had prayed for their five ladies, a love began to develop within these women that made them want to meet needs. They began to reach out to these families in love. One by one, these women began to come to Sunday School. They were in a Concentric Circle. They had a contact. They knew they would walk into the class and the one who had reached out to them would be there.

A Trip to the Hospital

One of the four ladies was concerned with a lady we will call Jan, who not only was having mental problems but also family problems. Jan came to Sunday School regularly for five weeks. One day after class, Jan came to Carolyn and said, "I just want you to know that I will be out of town next Sunday. We are going to visit my family out of state." As Jan talked, Carolyn wrote her name and phone number on a slip of paper, handed it to Jan, and she put it into her purse.

In two or three days, Carolyn received a phone call from the

hospital. Jan had taken an overdose of sleeping pills. When the
ambulance had come, Jan told the driver to get the sheet of
paper from her purse and to radio for Carolyn to come to get the
children at her house. She said she did not know whom else to
call.

Christ Becoming Real

A lady in Carolyn's class began to intercede for Jan. Jan
was able to begin to deal with her own problems as Christ
became real in her life. Within six months, she was able to begin
reaching out to meet other people's needs. She and her husband
were reunited, and they took vital roles in the church.

In only three months the class had at least twenty-five
members present each Sunday and had to find a larger meeting
place in the assembly area. From their survey, their intercessory
prayers, and building bridges, within seven months the class
averaged thirty-five to forty women each Sunday. That is what
can happen when a Sunday School gets really serious about
Concentric Circles—about loving—about meeting needs—about
intercession.

What About the Church?

Can you imagine what would happen if a whole church
began to take a survey, to intercede, to start working through
their Concentric Circles? We would go into the worship service
expecting, anticipating God's working in hearts and lives.

Dick, another of my students, went out to pastor a little
country church. It was one of those situations where the church
had been there forever, and they planned to remain there forever. But they did not plan to do anything.

When they were looking for a preacher, usually a student,
they hired him if they liked him. Then, if they changed their
minds, they would fire him.

Dick said, "Dr. Thompson, what should I do? I preach;
nothing happens. I want them to pray, but they do not want to;

they say they hired me to pray. I want them to go visiting; they do not want to go visiting because they say visiting is my job. These people could take the heart out of a hickory log. They do not want to do anything. But, they did want to have a 'meetin'.' "

I know the word is *meeting,* the word is *revival,* but they wanted a "meetin'." So I said, "Dick, why don't you share Concentric Cirlces with them?" He did.

After his presentation, one of the deacons said, "Preacher, I have a son who was married in this church last summer. He and his bride have not been back since. I had not even thought about it. I am going to put them down in my circles and pray for them."

Then a little grandmother came up to Dick and said, "You know, I have a granddaughter who is fourteen. She has never made a profession of faith. I am going to pray for her."

Several others told Dick that the message had reminded them of someone to pray for.

Well, this little church had its "meetin'." They also had seventeen professions of faith which doubled the size of their congregation! The people were so excited that they kept adding to their survey.

These who once could have taken the heart out of a hickory log were interceding, building bridges, confronting people, and learning what the word *disciple* means. This is revival. These people had caught the vision of their Jerusalem, their Judea, their Samaria, and their world and how the gospel moves through Concentric Circles.

6
Love Is—Meeting Needs

God designed human beings for love. From the Genesis to the Revelation, there is that one command from the Father—LOVE.

Deuteronomy 6:5 says, "You shall love the LORD your God with all your heart and with all your soul and with all your might."

In the New Testament, we are told that the first and greatest commandment is to love God with all our hearts and souls and minds (Matt. 22:37-38; Mark 12:30).

Now you might ask, "How do I love God?"

Love Demonstrated

One morning after a class in which we had been talking about *love is meeting needs,* one of my students, Rob, was walking down the hall to the elevator with me.

Rob said, "Dr. Thompson, I am not really sure I understand something. I understand what you are saying about *love is meeting needs* and that God wants to meet even the deepest need of people through me; but the first and great commandment is to love the Lord God with all our hearts, souls, and minds. The Bible says to love the Lord first, but Dr. Thompson, how do I love God? He doesn't have any needs. How am I going to show God that I love him?"

And I said, "My dear friend, Matthew 25:35-40 gives us the answer to that question. In this Scripture passage, Jesus says, 'I was hungry, and you gave Me *something* to eat; I was thirsty, and you gave Me drink; I was a stranger, and you invited Me in; naked, and you clothed Me; I was sick, and you visited Me; I was in prison, and you came to me.' And then Jesus said, 'to the extent that you did it to one of these brothers of Mine, *even* the least *of them,* you did it to Me.' "

How Do We Love God?

When you love people in Jesus' name, you are loving Jesus. When those who are precious to Jesus become precious to you, you are loving God with all of your *heart* and *soul* and *mind.* You are not really loving Jesus until you become a channel of his love in meeting needs. *Love is meeting needs.*

In Matthew 22:39 and Mark 12:31, we find that the second great commandment is, "YOU SHALL LOVE YOUR NEIGHBOR AS YOURSELF."

Loving the Unlovely

Remember, when Jesus becomes Lord of your life, you forfeit forever the right to choose whom you will love. You may say, "I just love the world." All right, do you love Jim?

"No," you say, "he is cantankerous. I don't love him."

Then what about Sue?

"Well, I love almost everybody but Sue."

The reason God leaves you in this clay house as long as he does is so that he can reach down to you and through you and reveal himself to a world. That is the reason you occupy space and take up oxygen. He wants to love through you. *Love is meeting needs.*

The Revelation of Love

"For God so loved the world, that he *gave* his only begotten Son, that whosoever believeth in him should not perish, but have everlasting life" (John 3:16, KJV). God loved us and he met our needs.

"God demonstrates His own love toward us, in that while

we were yet sinners, Christ died for us" (Rom. 5:8). Love is meeting needs. God wants to meet your needs, and he wants to meet the needs of others through you.

There are three Greek words that are translated "love." The first is *eros*. It is the sexual, passionate, fleshly love. There is nothing wrong with it. God designed it for you within the confines of marriage.

The second is the word *philia*. This is a love in which the quality of relationship is stressed. Are there some people you just like to be around? That is *philia*. It is a good love. It is a Christian love. It is a love of feeling, of emotion. It is good when you can say, "I not only love my wife but I like her too." This is the word we are talking about.

The third word for love in Scripture is *agape*. It is not necessarily based on feeling. It is pure, reasoned, logical volition. *Agape* means that here is a need; I am going to meet that need.

You say, "But I must *feel* something for people before I love them."

The Reason for Love

Let me ask you this. What kind of feeling did Jesus have when he died on the cross for us? It was not a feeling that sent him to the cross, dear friend. It was our need that sent him to the cross. He had a deep feeling for us, but the feeling came because he looked at our sin and he saw our deep need. That *agape* love transcended the agony of the cross. By his act he said, "I will meet your needs." He saw our need and met it.

Now do not tell me about winning the world if you cannot love your neighbor. Do not tell me about winning the world if you do not take time to meet the needs of your own child or spouse. You are to be a channel of love. Start in your "Jerusalem," your home.

Agape is meeting needs. I was a pastor for about twenty years. Many times about 5:30 in the afternoon I just did not get very excited about going visiting that evening. Have you ever felt that way? Of course, you have! But when those times come, what do we do? We say, "Lord Jesus, I love *You* and I am going visiting because I love you." It is an *agape* love.

How Do We Love People?

So we ask, "How do we love people?" We are to love people the same way God loves people—by meeting their needs.

"You have heard that it was said, 'YOU SHALL LOVE YOUR NEIGHBOR, and hate your enemy.' But I say to you, love your enemies, and pray for those who persecute you" (Matt. 5:43-44).

How do you love your enemies? What does God say? Find someone *you love* and *treat* your *enemy* the *very same way*. *Love is treating all people the very same way*. When Jesus becomes Lord of your life, you forfeit forever the right to choose whom you will love.

Love Is not Showing Favoritism

James 2:8-9 says that if you really keep the royal law found in Scripture, "YOU SHALL LOVE YOUR NEIGHBOR AS YOURSELF," you are doing right. But if you show favoritism, you sin and are convicted by the law as lawbreakers.

I am going to tell you a story from Matthew 5:45. Let us reverently pretend for a moment that you are the Lord. You have two fellows down here on earth who are both farmers. One of those farmers honors you. He says, "Lord, I love you." He gives of the increase of his ground, and he bows down and worships you.

But the other farmer across the fence disrespects you, takes your name in vain, does not give any of the increase back to you, and in every way abhors you.

Now if you were God—here comes our reaction—what would you do? You would give rain and sunshine to the fellow who loves you. Right? You would turn the other fellow's water off. Isn't that right? That is our natural reaction. But what did

Jesus say? "He causes His sun to rise on *the* evil and on *the* good, and sends rain on *the* righteous and on *the* unrighteous."

Out in your Concentric Circles, you are going to find all kinds of people who are not lovely. You work with them at the office, and they are just as cantankerous as they can be. They are not receptive to you, but you begin to pray: "Father, reveal to me their needs. Here I am. You know all the responsibilities I have; but wherever I go and whomever my life touches, I will be salt. I will be salt to touch and preserve, to help and heal and love."

When you find that person out there who is just impossible, you say, "Father, engineer circumstances in his life to draw him to you, to meet his need."

So we see that the genuine, God-given *agape* love does not depend on a feeling. *Feelings* fluctuate; *love* is stable. Love stems from a deep motivation. That motivation does not come from circumstances. That motivation must come totally disconnected from circumstances or it will not be profitable.

Genuine love does not depend on the person whom you are loving to return that love or to be receptive to that love, or to love first.

During our summer session last year, a young man came into my class and sat on the back row. Although I had one hundred students in the class, I spotted him. I thought, *I am going to have trouble with this student! I can just tell.*

Acting and Reacting

Well, one day as I talked to the class about reacting to circumstances, I said, "God will place you in circumstances in which he wants to love someone through you. If you do not react in *agape* love—depending on the Holy Spirit, abiding in the Word, trusting in him—you are going to blow it."

After class, Jerry came to me and said, "Dr. Thompson, your class is about to plow me under."

I asked, "What's the matter, Jerry?"

He said, "Well, you were talking to me [he personalized it] about God's drawing people into my Concentric Circles. You said he engineers circumstances to bring people into my life and how I respond either gives me the opportunity to share the gospel with them or lose it."

"That's right," I replied.

He said, "I think I blew it."

I said, "Tell me about it."

So Jerry told me this story.

"I work in Dallas and drive my motorbike to work each day. For the last two days as I have pulled into the parking lot, I have noticed a bike exactly like mine, only it does not have a mirror.

"When I came out to the parking lot last night, my mirror was missing. So I walked down to the other bike, and there it was. *My* mirror was on *his* bike. I knew it was my mirror because it was marked.

"I took my mirror off his bike and was so very angry that I flooded his bike. It did not hurt his bike, but it took about thirty minutes for him to start it.

"When I got home, the Lord really began to deal with me. What do I do?"

"Well, I am not sure, Jerry," I said. "What is the Holy Spirit telling you to do?"

Jerry turned and went off muttering in his beard, "That is what I thought you would say."

That was Friday. Jerry came back to class the next week and said, "May I share something with the class?

"Friday night, I went back to work and there was this fellow's bike. I said to myself, *I need to treat this fellow as if he were a dear friend and he has a need. Apparently his need is a mirror because he had stolen mine.* I went to the store and bought a mirror just like mine and put it on his bike. I also left a note. I said, 'I know you stole my mirror. I am the one who flooded your bike. But because of a relationship I have with Jesus Christ, he would not tolerate that attitude in my life.' I left the mirror and note with my name and phone number on it.

"That next night the fellow called me. He said, 'I have stolen many things in my life, but I have never received this kind of reaction. Can we talk?'

"That night in my apartment that guy got down on his knees and gave his life to Jesus."

God leads us, as he did Jerry, into circumstances. He leads *you* into circumstances with your family, your neighbors, the people at work, and everywhere you go so that he can reveal himself through you.

Now I realize that what I am suggesting is not practical in today's world, but it works! Let me ask you this, Who else is going to do it?

Jesus said, "Whoever shall force you to go one mile, go with him two" (Matt. 5:41).

Here again I have a very fertile imagination. I look out into a field and see a Jewish boy doing some pruning in the vineyard. It was a Roman law in those days that the soldiers could ask the Jews to carry their baggage for one mile.

A Roman soldier comes along and says, "Boy, come here. I want you to carry my baggage."

The infuriated Jewish boy, with white knuckles and clenched teeth, climbs over the fence. As he climbs over, he knocks some rocks off the fence, which angers him even more. If looks could kill! Well, he picks up the baggage but does not say a thing. When he comes to the end of that mile, he drops that baggage like a hot rock, turns on his heels, and returns to his work in the vineyard.

The next day the Roman soldier is coming back by that same vineyard. He looks out and sees who he thinks is the same boy and decides to aggravate him again.

The Roman soldier says, "Boy, come and carry my baggage again."

The boy looks up and says, "Good morning, sir," bolts the fence, picks up the baggage, and says, "What is your destination?"

The Roman soldier says, "I am going to Caesarea. I am going back to Rome."

"Do you have a family?" the boy asks.

"Yes," says the Roman soldier. "A wife and three children." The boy involves the Roman in conversation. They come to the end of the first mile. The Roman sees it; the Jewish boy ignores it.

Finally, the boy and the Roman soldier come to the end of the second mile. The boy says, "Well, I must get back to my work."

The Roman says, "Son, didn't you see the mile marker back there? You went two miles."

"Oh," the boys says, "I know. But my Master says, 'Whoever shall force you to go one mile, go with him two.' "

You say, "That is going to cost me."

I ask you, "Did it cost Jesus to go to the cross?"

Remember, love is action. It is doing. *Love is meeting needs.* Our attitude is formed on the immediacy of who is in control, Jesus or me? I form an attitude and out of that attitude, I react.

There is only one way we can be what Jesus wants us to be: by not agreeing with the old nature but by agreeing with him. That is submission to the authority of the King. When that happens, he is glorified, and people see Jesus in me. Agreeing with Jesus is not natural. It is supernatural.

Many of our opportunities to share the Lord are blocked and the Spirit of God is quenched because we react wrongly to circumstances. We react as the world reacts, and it just does not work.

You may ask, "What kind of love is this *agape* love?"

The Bible says, "Owe nothing to anyone except to love one another; for he who loves his neighbor has fulfilled *the* law" (Rom. 13:8). Go right down the Ten Commandments. You are not going to steal from someone you really love. You are not going to kill someone you love. Neither would you commit adultery against someone if there is a love relationship.

The Holiness of God

Sometimes we have to see the love of God, the white heat of the love of God, over against the literal holiness of God. God's love needs to be seen against his holiness.

When the great revival came in 1734, Jonathan Edwards had preached a series of sermons entitled, "The Justice of God in the Damnation of Sinners."

People saw for the first time the holiness of God. That was when revival came. God is a holy God. Genuine revival will never come in our land and we will never learn the great love of God until it is seen against his glorious holiness. He demands holy living. *Agape* is a sacred love.

What do I mean by sacred love? Well, remember Esau? The Scriptures say that Esau was a profane man. That does not necessarily mean that he was a "cusser." He probably was, but that is not what the Scriptures were talking about. It meant that nothing was sacred in Esau's life. In other words, everything had a price. His birthright, which should have been the most precious thing in his life, had a price.

We look at our secular society today. Everything has a price. Does your word have a price? My dad said to me, "Son, your word is your bond. I do not care what it costs you. Tell the truth. Your word must be sacred. It does not have a price."

When you distill it to its final essence, if love is not sacred, then it has a price. God's love does not have a price. It is pure. It will go to all lengths. It does not call for payment. It is sacred. It is holy.

The Resource of Meeting Needs

God's plan for your life is that his love flow through your life and reach out to others and meet their needs. You do not meet their needs out of your reservoir. You meet needs out of God's reservoir. Isn't that great? "Father, I want to be a channel. The reason you leave me in this clay house, in this body, as long as you do is to flow through me and reach out and take hold of people and build a relationship to them, a relationship cemented by *agape* love." So I develop a relationship with anyone and God draws that person to himself through that relationship. So we have our Concentric Circles. We have our relationships.

Some people in our Concentric Circles may not be lovable. You may say, "I cannot love that person." But remember, God says that *he* loves him. If we are going to be in agreement with God, then we must love whom he loves and meet his needs.

You do not get your motivation for telling the world about Jesus from a love for people. You get your motivation from your love for Jesus.

The most important encounter that Jesus had with the apostle Peter after the resurrection was at the morning seaside breakfast.

"Peter, do you love me? Feed my sheep."

Now Peter could have replied, "Lord, I do not love sheep. I am a fisherman."

And the Lord could have said, "Peter, I did not ask if you loved sheep. I asked if you loved *me*" (see John 21:15-17).

Seeing the needs of humanity will never be enough motivation to love the world. There are many altruistic people who go out to meet the needs of the world by giving out of their own resources until they are drained dry. Their resources are not adequate. So their idealism turns to disillusionment. Often the disillusionment turns to bitterness, then bitterness causes broken relationships. A case in point is the altruistic preacher who gives and gives until his own well runs dry. His *motive* is to meet others' needs so that he may have his own needs met.

Others sense his real motive and turn from it. The preacher leaves the ministry, disturbed and empty, feeling frustration and failure.

The Resource of Love

Little does this frustrated person realize that he is not the source to meet others' needs, but only the *channel*. A person needs to realize that his resources and his love are from God, and he must draw them from him. Otherwise a person practices a humanism that cannot stand up under the demands of today's world.

Our love for God must precede our love for the lost. If we love God, we will love whom he loves. To love without action, without meeting needs, is not love. Every time you find God loving man, God is meeting needs.

When you look out through your Concentric Circles, you will say: "Father, here I am. I go to your great reservoir of love, and I depend upon that great funnel of your love to flow through me to meet the needs of those around me."

If you would begin to meet the needs of those in your family, you would get your own needs met. Sometimes we say, "No one loves me, and no one is meeting my needs. Why should I meet anybody else's?"

Well, I will tell you. It is the genius of the gospel. You go to the cross and die to self. Every Christian needs to work through Romans 6 and 7. You are to die to self and then let Jesus become alive in you. Then he funnels his love through you.

As you are meeting needs, there is a wonderful by-product. When you love other people, God gives dividends.

The Results of Love

One night, years ago when I was pastoring, a teenage girl came blasting into my office. She was a redheaded, vivacious, never-hit-the-ground-type of personality. She came charging in, plunked down in a chair, cried a few crocodile tears, and sobbed, "Brother Oscar, I am so unhappy."

"Tell me about it," I answered.

She replied, "Nobody loves me."

Do you know what my pastoral response was? You will think this is so professorial and so dignified. I said, "Good grief, Brenda. I know your parents. I know they are busy with their new business, but they love you. I know your friends. They love you."

"No they don't," she replied. "Nobody loves me. I could just die and nobody cares."

I said, "Brenda, let me ask you a question. Are you a Christian?"

She looked shocked and said, "Brother Oscar, you know I am a Christian."

I said, "Brenda, who told you someone was supposed to love you anyway!"

"What do you mean?" she asked.

I said, "In the economy of God, you have been created by him as a channel for love to flow through you to others. The trouble is that you want the flow to go the wrong way. That is the reason you are miserable. When the flow of love is going the right way, as you were designed, you will not feel this way. You are supposed to do the loving. The person who always has to have the stream of love flowing inward is going to become a stagnant pool. Brenda, I believe you are stagnant.

"You go find some people out there and meet their needs. You do not have to feel great about them. You do not have to feel good about loving them. You do not have to have any feeling. From the heart you just make a commitment, 'Dear God, whatever people you put in my path, I am going to meet their needs.'

"Now," I said, "tomorrow I want you to make yourself available to the Lord Jesus. I want you to get alone with him. In the morning I want you to love somebody. Who is there out there that would be really difficult for you to love?"

Immediately she replied, "Judy."

"Who is Judy?" I asked.

"Judy is a freshman," Brenda said. "She is just dumb. She rides the bus with me, and," she continued, "she just bugs me."

I said, "Well, what is the problem?"

Brenda said, "I have to ride with her forty-five minutes every day. She crawls on the bus and it is chatter, chatter, chatter. I just do not want to listen to that freshman. She just latches on to me. I am a senior."

"Well, out of your immense senior wisdom, why don't you meet some of the needs of this lowly little freshman's ignorance." And we both laughed.

"Assignment number one is for you to love Judy. That is my prescription. Now, I have to go to a meeting. I will see you Sunday."

I realize that I was using direct counseling, but it worked.

Well, Brenda came back Sunday, and this was her story.

"I got on the bus Thursday morning. No sooner than I sat down, here came Judy. She sat down right beside me. It just really bugged me. I said, 'Lord, I am going to meet her need if it kills me.' The best thing I thought I could do was just listen. So I turned to her, and for the first time I looked at her while she was talking to me. As I looked at her, I began to see a little face I had never noticed before. I realized that underneath all that chatter was a hurting little girl.

"As we continued to talk, I asked, 'Judy, tell me about your brothers and sisters and mom and dad.' She became very still and quiet and was silent for awhile. Finally she said, 'Brenda, my mom and dad are getting a divorce, and I am so scared. We are going to have to move, and my whole world is coming apart.' "

Brenda said, "Brother Oscar, in that moment I just listened. That is all I did, but I felt the love of God wanting to meet that little girl's needs through me. I put my arm around her, and we talked until we arrived at school.

"After getting off the bus, Judy put her books on the ground and put her arms around me and said, 'Oh, Brenda, I just love you.' "

Now do you have someone in your Concentric Circles who "bugs you"? Perhaps they have a deep problem. Perhaps you need to reach out and be sensitive to that person's need. Who is going to help him if you don't? Let me tell you a story.

The Joys of a Prince Albert Tobacco Can

Years ago there was a one-room schoolhouse out in the country. The school taught the first through the tenth grades.

A little boy in that one-room school was always into something. He had a Prince Albert tobacco can, not because he smoked but to put his little treasures in.

Those of you who have never enjoyed having a Prince Albert tobacco can have never really lived. You can put all kinds of "worms, snails, puppy dog tails" in a Prince Albert tobacco can.

At recess one day, the little boy found a bumble bee. He put it into his can, and he was delighted. It was so much fun. He could hear ZZZZZZZZZZZZZZZZZ in that can; but then the bell rang, and it was time to go back to work.

The little boy put the can in the hip pocket of his jeans and went to class. He could hear ZZZZZZZ.

Well, this little boy did not understand the physics of a crimped can in a tight jean hip pocket. As a result, when he sat down, the bee was able to get out of the can. The bee was very disturbed about his close quarters and when he was able to escape from the can, but not from the close confines of the pocket, he began immediately to register his displeasure at such confinement.

The little boy began to hop around on the back row. That bee was really getting to him, if you know what I mean.

Seeing him hop around on that back row, the teacher demanded, "Johnny, what is the matter with you? Sit still!" But he could not sit still. He just kept jumping around. And she said again, "Johnny, sit still!"

To which Johnny replied, "Teacher, there are things going on back here that you don't know nothing about."

They Are Hurting

Johnny's explanation may not be couched in the best grammar, but I believe you get the picture. When you are reaching out to people who "just bug you" or you get a bad reaction from loved ones or friends, you pray for them. They may have things going on in their lives that you know nothing about. They may be in despair. They need your love, not your striking back at them.

Be sensitive to the needs of those about you. There may be things going on that you do not know anything about, and you may be able to reach in and meet their needs.

Back to Brenda. She said, "Brother Oscar, after I had met Judy's need, I went around all day looking for someone else to love. I arrived at home that afternoon and went in the front door. There sat Kim, my little sister, a seventh grader. She was watching 'Popeye.' The house looked like the aftermath of the Third World War. My little sister bugs me too."

Brenda said she turned to her little sister and said, "Kim, have you seen that program before?"

"Seventeen times," Kim answered.

Brenda asked, "Do you have any homework?"

"Yes, I have algebra, but I do not know how to do it."

"Well," said Brenda, "suppose you spread your homework out on the kitchen table, and I will help you with it."

Brenda said that her little sister looked at her like a calf looks at a new gate and exclaimed, "*You* are going to help *me* with my homework?"

"Yes," Brenda replied, "I will be back in a minute."

Kim muttered, "I do not believe this!"

Brenda continued, "I sat down, and Kim and I worked through the algebra; and I explained the problems that she did not understand. Then I suggested that we clean *her* room."

Brenda told me that they cleaned Kim's room and then cleaned the rest of the house. The girls then prepared the evening meal. Their parents usually arrived around 7:00.

When their parents arrived, there was the clean house and a hot meal on the table waiting for them. The girls almost had to get the smelling salts to revive them. As the family ate, they relaxed and enjoyed being together.

After eating, Brenda showered, dressed, and left on a date.

"When I came home and had dressed for bed, my mother came into my room and sat on my bed and said, 'Honey, I do not know what changed your attitude today. You have been so helpful to all of us. I cannot let you go to sleep tonight without telling you two things. Your little sister came in tonight before she went to bed and said that she really did love her big sister. You know, your dad and I have been so very busy trying to make our new business a success, but we just wanted you to know we love you too.' "

Brenda sat in my office and cried. She said, "Brother Oscar, all this time it has been *me, my, mine.* I have been trying to get my status in the world and struggling with my peer group. I have learned that when the flow of love is outward I am meeting the needs of others, and my own needs get met too."

Do you feel isolated? Do you feel that nobody cares about you, nobody loves you, and you get "the blues"? Let me give you a prescription. Go out in your Concentric Circles and meet someone else's needs.

Now do not go and comfort someone by telling him about all of your problems. That would be like the two fellows at the Golden Gate Bridge. One fellow was up on the bridge, getting ready to jump. The other fellow thought, *I believe I can talk him out of it.* So he walked up on the bridge. After they had talked for about forty-five minutes, both of them jumped! That is not what I have in mind. God has loved you. Now you go out and love somebody else. I have discovered that the happiest people in the world are those who are the channel of God's love. Love is meeting needs.

Let's Review

Let's review some of the basic and necessary things we have discovered in Concentric Circles.

The key to a fulfilled life is relationships. Things do not satisfy—relationships do. The most important word in the English language is *relationship.* The first relationship is with the Father. When he becomes Lord of our lives, we forfeit forever the right to choose whom we will love. When he becomes Lord, he releases his love in us to build right relationships.

God established the home before any other institution. The home is the basic institution in which God seeks to teach the sacredness of relationships and how to establish and nourish a relationship. The home is the *only institution* designed to teach relationships. When this institution fails, a child is left mentally, emotionally, and spiritually crippled for life.

The home under God should be the place to learn about relationships—husband and wife, parent and child, child to child. Here is where a person learns to love—learns to meet needs. A helpless baby placed in the hands of parents matures and develops their ability to love, to meet needs. A child is taught to submit his wayward, self-centered will to the will of the parents. Here selfishness, which is the root of sin, matures into a discipline to build relationships and meet the needs of *others.*

God has designed the home to be the school of relationships. The dearest, the closest, the most intimate human relationship that must exist is between husband and wife. Then through that close relationship we teach our children about relationships. This is our own school of relationships.

Now this relationship is linked to another relationship at the church. All of these relationships become the body of Christ. We need one another.

We know that God wants to meet our needs. He builds beautiful relationships in the body of Christ.

Jesus came to earth to meet our deepest need. He died on the cross to redeem the earth to himself. He ascended to heaven, and he left the body of Christ on earth to go out and enlarge the body and strengthen the body.

Let's say the church is the divine hospital. The world is so very full of sickness. Many, many people come to the hospital for help, and every church that is doing what it needs to be doing realizes that all of us need help. We continually need help. We come and come and come for help, and we receive it. The only tragedy is that, if we do not mature and join the hospital staff and start meeting other people's needs, we become a liability and the flow is always going inward. So we stagnate, and that hurts us.

After we have come for help and have received it, God wants us to go out and build relationships with others. Then we will become part of the helping staff. As we reach out to meet another's needs, we find our own needs are met.

Love is
NOT a word of emotion,
NOT a word of feeling.

Rather, love is
A word of reason,
A word of volition or will,
A word of action,
Love is doing!

Love *builds* relationships;
Love *maintains* relationships;
Love *fulfills* relationships;
Love *initiates* relationships.

Love is meeting needs!

7
Overcoming Barriers

A barrier is anything in the Christian's life-style that hinders his sharing the gospel with another.

What Is the Gospel?

The meaning for the English word *gospel* is "good news." It is used seventy-six times in the New Testament. When you anglicize the Greek word, you have *euangelion.* Notice the "eu" on the front of the word. In Greek, "eu" always means good. *Euphonos* means good sound. *Eulogos* means good word. Actually the Old English word was *godspel* if you look up *gospel* in *Webster's Third Unabridged Dictionary.* As *godspel* was translated, it became known as "gospel."

It only seems right that any good news we have, we would want to share with those who are closest to us. These people are those with whom we have developed a relationship.

Hiding the Good News

Sometimes we Christians become artificial and, therefore, hypocritical. We want to carry the good news out to Person X somewhere, but we do not want to carry it to the ones around us. You may say, "But it is hard to witness to people I really know." If what you say is true, the relationships you have are not real. In reality your love and concern for yourself is greater than your love for those closest to you.

Broken Relationships

So let's look at three barriers that can keep us from sharing the good news in our Concentric Circles. *First,* we may have bro-

102

ken relationships with those around us. Ruptured relationships hinder the movement of the Spirit of God within Christians' lives. They neutralize our witness and its importance. Broken relationships shut off the divine well that can flow to all our world. To keep the divine well flowing, we Christians need to right all broken relationships.

Overcoming Fear

The *second* barrier in sharing the good news with those we know is fear of rejection or fear of failure.

In order to understand fear, we need to see what God's Word says about it. In 2 Timothy 1:7 we find that fear does not come from God: "For God has not given us a spirit of timidity [fear], but of power and love and discipline."

Also we are given a command to witness without fear; "but sanctify Christ as Lord in your hearts, always *being* ready to make a defense to everyone who asks you to give an account for the hope that is in you, yet with gentleness and reverence; and keep a good conscience so that in the thing in which you are slandered, those who revile your good behavior in Christ may be put to shame" (1 Pet. 3:15-16).

But to hear something is one thing; to apply it is another. When God gives us insight into himself and his will, we are put in double jeopardy. In other words, God holds us responsible for what he teaches us. If he gives us a truth about himself and we do not obey it, we are hurt spiritually. One of my students honestly admitted, "Then I just want to be ignorant."

But that student's choice is not the answer either. We need to get our ruptured relationships righted and then claim 2 Timothy 1:7 and agree with it. We need to step forward and be obedient without being intimidated.

"He who has My commandments and keeps them, he it is who loves Me; and he who loves Me shall be loved by My Father, and I will love him, and will disclose Myself to him" (John 14:21).

Walking in Agreement. If you agree with what God has told you about what he wants you to do and you obey it, God has said he will disclose or make himself conspicuous or real in your life. When Jesus reveals his will for your life and you obey him, he becomes conspicuous. He becomes real.

The times in my life when Jesus has been real have been those times when I have, out of sheer obedience, said, "Father, I do not know how, why, or what, but I *will* obey you."

I cannot measure obedience to God on a slide rule. I do not plan to put it in some theory. I am just saying that it is God's nature to become conspicuous or real in our lives if we obey him.

Building Your House on a Rock. I will never forget when the seminary invited me to teach, and Carolyn and I moved to Fort Worth. Soon after, we decided to build our own home. We designed it, selected our lot, and began to build. The Lord said to build your house upon a rock, and I did. With grubbing hoe and pick, one of my dear students and I began to dig the foundation.

One day, leaning on the pick and perspiring, that student said to me as we labored together, "Doc, I am really glad about one thing."

"What?" I replied.

"I am glad you did not decide to build a basement."

One night we were working late to finish digging the pit for the fireplace. The house has two stories and stacked fireplaces: one in the family room and one in our master bedroom upstairs. We had to dig down five feet into the rock to put in enough concrete and steel to support the weight of a double fireplace.

Well, that cold windy night, dressed in an old trench coat and hard hat, I dug while Carolyn held the light. A police officer, new on the beat, stopped his car, beamed his light on us, rolled down his window, and yelled, "What are you doing?"

Carolyn looked at me, and I shouted back to him, "Digging a grave!"

You talk about getting attention. The officer jumped out of his car to have a look as we explained the situation. We became friends. He stopped each night to check on our progress.

But later that night we finally went to the house we were renting. We went straight to bed. I was exhausted. Carolyn had already collapsed, and the house was very, very still. All of a sudden, I heard the drip of a faucet.

If I will be really still, maybe Carolyn will hear it and get up and turn it off, I thought.

Well, she did not. Instead I felt a gentle, little hand touch me and say, "Honey, please turn off the faucet."

I want to tell you something, friend. That dripping water was the most conspicuous thing in the room. I could not divert my attention from it. When we pray, "Father, I want you to be conspicuous; I want to sense your presence," God will be as real to us as that dripping faucet was to me.

As you walk through each day of your life, Jesus wants to be conspicuous. He wants to be so conspicuous that you cannot ignore him or make any decision without him. That is how conspicuous and real Jesus wants to be in every Christian's life.

Meeting the One Who Is Love

And finally, the *third* barrier hindering you from reaching out to love people in your Concentric Circles is that perhaps you have never met the One who is love. Have you met Jesus?

With our five senses we perceive the world. We lock into our minds as knowledge what our five senses tell us. We can know about God mentally. Consequently, many people only know *about* God. They can give many concepts about God, but they do not know God.

My *body* makes me world-conscious, my *mind* makes me self-conscious, and my *spirit* makes me God-conscious. But if my spirit is dead in trespasses and sin, a holy God cannot be there. I still have a spirit, but it is dead toward God. In the new birth, God breaks through and comes to dwell in me and makes me alive spiritually. I am then born from above.

The authority of the Christian life is no longer physical.

When a Christian is born from above, the Spirit of God dwells in that person's spirit, flows through his mind, and moves through his body. Then we Christians, "present [our] bodies a living and holy sacrifice" (Rom. 12:1). Why?

So that "from his innermost being shall flow rivers of living water" (John 7:38).

To what?

You are the channel through which the Holy Spirit wants to move and manifest himself to the world, and that happens when a man is born again. He is alive to God.

Are You Hurting?

Perhaps you have deep needs in your own life. You are hurting. Remember that because God loves you, there is not a need in your life that he has not already made provision for. The *greatest* provision is that your sins be forgiven. You can join the church, lead a good moral life, help people, give money to the church; but these actions cannot take away your sin.

Jesus Christ entered history and *died* to save us from our sins. He paid the price of death for our sins so that we can be forgiven. *Jesus' death* is *God's provision for our need.* Because of him, we have eternal life.

Religion is good views about God. The *gospel* is good news from God. *Reformation* is man's doing. *Transformation* is what God does. When the Holy Spirit sheds the love of God in our hearts, he puts his ministry of love into action in our lives.

As a Christian what should be the theme of your life? What should you be as God's servant?

Therefore if any man is in Christ, *he* is a new creature; the old things passed away; behold, new things have come. Now all *these* things are from God, who reconciled us to Himself through Christ, and gave us the ministry of reconciliation, namely, that God was in Christ reconciling the world to Himself, not counting their trespasses against them, and He has committed to us the word of reconciliation. Therefore, we are ambassadors for Christ, as though God were entreating through us; we beg you on behalf of Christ, be reconciled to God. He made Him who knew no sin *to be* sin on our behalf, that we might become the righteousness of God in Him (2 Cor. 5:17-21).

These verses are the gospel in a nutshell. They tell how God brought us to himself through Christ's dying on the cross to pay for our sin. They reveal how we are responsible for sharing the good news of how he reconciled us and how he wants us to reconcile others, through Christ to himself.

We are to share compassionately the good news of Jesus with lost people in the power of the Holy Spirit for the purpose of winning them to Jesus Christ as their Savior and Lord. They, in turn, then will share him with others. This is the *ministry* of reconciliation and the *word* of reconciliation. Therefore, God tells us that we are ambassadors for Christ.

What Is an Ambassador?

An ambassador is one who represents someone other than himself at the court of another. My beloved friend, if you are a Christian, you are an ambassador of Jesus Christ. This should be the biblical motif with which you approach your life-style.

Wherever you go, you represent Jesus. At the office, you are an ambassador for Christ. Teaching school, running a business, buying your groceries, wherever, you are an ambassador for Christ. You represent the person of Jesus Christ everywhere you go.

Have you ever seen someone who by his attitudes, selfishness, unthoughtfulness, and self-centeredness did not represent Christ well? How tragic!

Christians represent Jesus in every area of living. Wherever Christians go, twenty-four hours a day, we are ambassadors for Jesus Christ.

When Should Your Ministry Begin?

Some people have the wrong idea about a Christian ministry. They say that when I learn this or become that way, I will start my ministry. I have students who say, "When I graduate and my ministry begins . . ." No! Your ministry is today. Do not waste a minute. God takes you where you are, and you are to begin your ministry NOW.

You will not have a ministry if you do not have it now. If you will be faithful over a few things, God will make you ruler over many (Matt. 25:23). So, remember that your ministry is not out there somewhere; it is now. The moment Jesus comes into your heart, your ministry begins. He wants to be free to work through you.

The Highest Calling

The highest calling in the world is *not* to preach the gospel. The highest calling in the world is to be a *Christian*. Consequently, every one of us, in the reality of the word, is a minister and has a ministry within his own Concentric Circles.

Many people say, "God just did not intend for me to be a super Christian." That is right! He did not intend for you to be a super anything. He expects you to be you, in whom he dwells and fills.

"If I become a Spirit-filled Christian," many Christians say, "I will have to be a missionary or preacher or do something special." No! Some of the greatest Spirit-filled Christians I know sell parts in a hardware store, own businesses, teach in schools, or sell houses. They never preach a sermon, *per se;* they live one every day.

Being filled with the Spirit does not make an introvert an extrovert. Many people think they should have some kind of personality change, but Jesus does not want to reproduce his personality in you. He wants to use your personality and reproduce *his character* in *your personality.* He wants to take you and reproduce his life in you.

Your Everyday Life-style Is to Reflect Jesus

Some fellows are able evangelists in the pulpit and have had many decisions for the Lord in their services. Yet, I have watched these same men act rudely toward a waitress or a sales-person and be first-class, carnal Christians. A Christian has no excuse for this. What does the world see? Does the world see Jesus?

The essence of the walk in Jesus Christ is his wanting to produce his character within the Christian. If you are a Christian, you have a ministry; and that ministry will be wherever you are. As you go through life, God wants to reach the world around you. He wants to love *your* world through you and to draw it to him. If you let barriers hinder you from doing this, little else that you accomplish in life matters. Your life will be desperately empty.

So every believer has his Jerusalem. In your Concentric Circles you find yours. It is not like anyone else's, is it? You have a Judea. Your Judea is not like anyone else's Judea. You have a Samaria. The Jews did not like the Samaritans, and you probably have people in your Samaria you do not like. But you do not *have* to *like them* to *love them*. In effect God says, "You meet the needs of those Samaritans; whatever they are, you meet them." Also, you have an uttermost part of the earth that God will draw into your circles.

Walking in Obedience

Many people lose the joy of their salvation because they do not walk in obedience with the Lord. Barriers form, and they let those barriers defeat them. Do you want Jesus to be real to you? Write down John 14:21, and commit it to memory. "He who has My commandments and keeps them, he it is who loves Me; and he who loves Me shall be loved of My Father, and I will love him, and will disclose Myself to him." Jesus was saying that he will make himself real.

Jesus Reveals Himself to You

Now I want to show you something more. Your searching for Jesus is not self-disclosure. He reveals himself. He makes himself real. Do you want Jesus to be real to you? Then obey him. The times in your life when Jesus was real were the times when you have faced a major decision and you decided to do it his way. You must say, "Father, I do not care what it costs. I do not care what I have to do."

You cannot put this on a slide rule. You cannot really explain it to anyone else, but Christ will become real in your life. It should be your walk every day. The man who walks with God every day has the reality of his presence as God manifests himself. This is God's promise, as recorded in John 14:21.

God's command is to, "Go therefore and make disciples of all nations" (Matt. 28:19).

We say, "Well, if we baptize a hundred thousand more next year than we did this year, we will rejoice." But this is no criteria since God's criteria is to "make disciples of all nations." But you are not responsible for *anybody* except *everybody* in your Concentric Circles. Why? This is simple enough. God has enough grace to save all of them and meet all of their needs. All you do is be faithful and available.

Obedience to Him

God is alive and well in you. But is he in control? Are there barriers that you have not overcome? Is he free to do all that he wants to do? Are you obedient to him? John 14:21 says that if you are obedient, he will make himself real to you.

Jesus needs to be real in your life. If he is not as real as he used to be, perhaps you need to go back and check the original problem, obedience. What did he tell you to do? What was the last point at which you disobeyed him?

Perhaps the problem of disobedience comes because of a ruptured relationship. Matthew 6:14-15 says, "If you forgive men for their transgressions, your heavenly Father will also forgive you. But if you do not forgive men, then your Father will not forgive your transgressions."

God lays down the law here about ruptured relationships.

We do not grieve over them. We just move.

I tell my young preachers that the problem with some of us is that we go out into a church and immediately rupture a relationship somewhere. Have you ever heard of the little word *pride?* Because we have so much pride, we will not admit we are wrong. Perhaps the other person was wrong, but we are to be the initiators of reconciliation.

If we allow our pride to run rampant, along will come another rupture and another. Eventually, as a result of all these ruptured relationships with people around us, we do not pastor anymore. We rupture enough relationships so that we have to move to another church. Then the cycle starts all over again. When will we learn that we are to be the initiators of reconciliation because God is the initiator of reconciliation?

Take an inventory of your life. You will find that your happiest days were those days of good relationships; the days of agony were those days of broken relationships.

You see, your relationships can make you the happiest person in the world or they can make you the most devastated. Why? The answer is that God has made us to have relationships.

What Really Makes You Happy

Things do not make you happy, although the world has bought the concept that they do. Things may excite you for a moment, but they will not make you happy. Then what does make you happy? Think back to chapter 1. That which satisfies the deepest longing of your being is a relationship with someone.

But remember, when we build a relationship with someone, we do not build that relationship on our conditions. Our conditions are always changing. We must build relationships on God's conditions.

Relationships satisfy. They meet our needs. Have you ever seen a lonely person? Have you ever been lonely? Have you ever been around someone who really loves and cares for you? This satisfies.

As we build relationships, we need to say, "Father, I will come to you on your conditions." As this relationship with God is established vertically, out of it we can establish many lasting, meaningful relationships horizontally.

I ask you, are there ruptures in your relationships? Are there barriers between you and someone else? Why? Are there people you cannot get along with? Why? Are there people who irritate you? Of course. How do you deal with them? Remember, we are to be the initiators of reconciliation.

The Balanced Life

Remember in chapter 2 when we talked about the balance of self? We saw that guilt pushes us down, so we seek to justify ourselves by blaming other people. Then that inferiority complex comes into full bloom, and we become achievers so that we can stand above our group and say, "I am the best there is." Then after we have achieved, boredom sets in; we are not fulfilled.

The only place we can actually find balance is at the cross. It is there that we do not have to blame anyone else. It is at the cross that we can be achievers, but the purpose for our achievement is for Jesus Christ to be Lord.

Something in Our Nature Cries Out for Fellowship

In the relationships of life, there must be an inner relationship. We cannot go off somewhere by ourselves. However, if we cannot get along with people, going off by ourselves may seem best. But we will not be fulfilled because something in our nature cries out for fellowship. We have caused barriers in our relationships with others.

Rare is the individual who wants to be a loner. In being a loner, a person loses the purpose for existence because God wants to reveal his character through a Christian's life. He does this by loving through you within a relationship with others.

John said, "What we have seen and heard we proclaim to you also, that you also may have fellowship with us; and indeed

our fellowship is with the Father, and with His Son Jesus Christ"
(1 John 1:3).

Forming an Attitude About Someone

Now let's say someone hits us in our circumstances. We
immediately spin around and form some kind of opinion about
him. That opinion becomes an attitude. The basis for that attitude will flow out of one of two natures. The natures are the first
Adam and the second Adam.

That first Adam says, "You hit me, and I am going to hit you
back." That is the reaction of *me, my,* and *mine.*

What does this cause? A ruptured relationship—a running
battle with someone. Has that ever happened between you and
your spouse? What about your children? What about at work or
at church?

Don't Be Troubled Over Circumstances

You do not have to be frustrated or anxious or troubled by
circumstances that come your way. Since nothing can come into
the life of a believer without God's permission, it comes with his
grace to deal with it.

But how do we appropriate God's grace? One day at a time.
"As thy days, so shall thy strength be" (Deut. 33:25).

Jesus said, "If anyone wishes to come after Me, let him
deny himself, and take up his cross, and follow Me" (Matt.
16:24). This must be done daily. But there is the problem. Most
of our lives are crucified between two thieves, *yesterday* and
tomorrow. We never live today. But the time to live is now. It is
today.

You Must Repent. Jesus said, "Unless you repent, you will
all likewise perish" (Luke 13:3). To repent means to change
one's attitude toward God, toward sin, and toward others. God
demands this. If our attitudes change, our life-styles will change
also.

My Earthly Father. My father was a wise, very quiet Texas

rancher. His word was his bond. I never heard him utter a blasphemous word, and he was a total Christian.

Dad wore big, black boots with his khaki pants tucked into them. He said that a rancher could tuck one pant's leg in for every seventy-five cows he owned. His black belt with the "W.O.T." initialed gold buckle was the one my mother gave him when they were married. With grey shirt, black, batwing tie, and Stetson hat, he rode the pasture.

I said, "Dad, a tie? It is hot!"

"Looks good," he said.

I would ask, "Who is looking? The cows?" This was my father. This was W. O. Thompson.

My father often told me to do things. If I did the task, but not well, he would say, "Son, you need to give more thought . . ." He did not chastise me for the way I did things. He was not as concerned about how I did something as he was about my attitude toward doing it.

If my attitude was not good, he would say, "I do not like your attitude. Change it." Friend, that meant *change it.* He would say, "You are in control of your attitude. You change it *now!*"

"Yes, sir."

Now when God tells you or me to repent, he wants a change of attitude. He wants it now.

Are You Sure God Loves You?

Several years ago I was diagnosed as having a disease that was expected to take my life within weeks. A student stood at the foot of my hospital bed and said, "Dr. Thompson, if this were to happen to me, I think I would be very bitter toward God. Look at all you have sought to do for him."

But I said, "Wait a minute, dear friend; you are not sure God loves you."

"Oh, yes, I am sure God loves me," he said.

"No," I said. "You are not sure God loves you because

when you are sure God loves you, you realize that perfect love casts out all fear. Nothing can ever come into the life of a Christian without God's permission. And if God permits it, then he will give the grace and strength to deal with it."

Whatever our circumstances, if we seek God, he will begin to show us that we can rest in his love. Then anything that comes into our lives can be used for his glory.

"Father, as we reach out into our Concentric Circles, show us the barriers in our lives that need to be overcome. Help us be obedient to you and take comfort in your love."

8
Building Bridges

Now that you have done your survey, have begun to intercede, and made yourself available to God, you will want to build bridges to people by reaching out in love and showing them that you care. The apostle Paul said, "I have become all things to all men, that I may by all means save some" (1 Cor. 9:22). In other words, Paul tried to identify with the needs of individuals.

Communication is not only what I say to you but it is also what you hear me say. A person knows I care when I get on his wave length.

Let's talk first about actual times to build bridges. Probably some of the best times to build relationships with people are to rejoice with them when they rejoice and to stand with them in times of stress.

Times of Joy

Having a Baby

One way to touch someone's life that has ordinarily been closed is to show him attention and consideration at the time of the birth of a baby. I have stood in a hospital and looked through the glass at some beautiful, little horrid face. Do you know what I mean? You tell that person how beautiful his baby is. There are beautiful babies, then there are beautiful babies who are not beautiful. I think if ever there is a time when God forgives us for lying, it is at the birth of a baby. How many times I have stood at the baby window in the hospital with a couple. I have stood looking at my own. What a wonderful, warm time to build a bridge!

We all laugh at the crazy behavior of fathers when time comes to go to the hospital. I remember Carolyn telling me about 10:30 one night, "Honey, I think we had better go to the hospital." Well, we went. As they asked us questions at the nurses' station, I could not think of my name, Carolyn's name, or our address. But at the hospital they all knew me; so one of the nurses escorted me to the nearest chair. Then she asked Carolyn the rest of the information. I thought Carolyn was going to have the baby before they finished getting the information. But Damaris was not born until the next afternoon at 1:37. There is no other time like the birth of a baby.

I have talked with new fathers as we both stood looking through that glass window at a precious little life. At times we have talked about the overwhelming responsibility of being parents. I tried to emphasize, "That is a great little life. Do you realize that God has given you the most important gift you will ever have?"

Weddings

Another good time to build bridges is at the time of marriage. Reach out and be helpful. Pastors and staff members, do not miss this opportunity to build bridges. Be sure there is a time of counseling before the marriage. You may tell the couple, "This is one of the most important decisions you will ever make. Therefore, it is imperative that you know some of the things that will make you happy."

Through the years as a pastor, I have told couples in our counseling sessions before their marriages, "For a marriage to be whole and all that you want it to be, all of the parts of the puzzle must fit."

I believe that the key to a successful marriage is intimacy. When you think of intimacy, you usually think of physical intimacy. But there is much more.

To have a biblical marriage, intimacy *must* exist on three

levels. *Mental-emotional-intellectual intimacy* is the *first*. Intimacy at this level means that no one on the face of this earth is closer to you than your mate. Do you want your marriage to be in trouble? Then you let *anyone* get closer to you than your mate. If you depend upon someone else more than you do your mate, if you want to share all of your deep thoughts with someone else *more* than you do with your mate, then there is a problem.

If you do have a problem in your marriage, take the first step. Begin to communicate. Talk about every problem, and do not let resentment and pride build up. Count the costs. The stakes are high because your marriage is in the balance. But when that communication is flowing and the warmth and love is there, two people cannot be happier. This kind of bond cannot be broken.

I can share with Carolyn when I cannot share with anyone else. My daughter, Damaris, and I are very close. We have a very special relationship, but it is different from the relationship that Carolyn and I share. Someday I want Damaris to have this same kind of very special relationship with her husband, and I pray that there will be no closer person on the face of the earth than those two are to each other.

Second, a biblical marriage must have *spiritual intimacy*. You are a spiritual being. Marriage is a holy triangle between a man, a woman, and God with God's love flowing through the man to the woman and God's love flowing from the woman to the man. It is a forgiving, redemptive, sharing kind of love.

The key word in marriage is *intimacy*. If you have a problem discuss it. Be open. Be mature. Work through your problems. Until a couple really communicates about a problem and works through it, that same problem will flare up all through their married life. Take your problems to the Lord. Nothing is too big to be worked out at the foot of the cross.

The *third* level is *physical intimacy*. All three levels of intimacy are essential to a strong, fulfilling marriage. If there is a problem in one of the first two levels of intimacy, physical intimacy will not be all it should be. Some people marry only for physical intimacy. When it ceases to satisfy, they move on; but in marriage after marriage, they will never find lasting fulfillment without all three levels of intimacy.

Intimacy comes through a relationship. Sometimes I say to couples, "I am not as interested in your becoming church members as in your becoming a success. Your attitudes toward your marriage and the basis upon which you build your marriage is going to make the difference in whether you succeed or not."

For a marriage to be all it needs to be, both husband and wife need to have a close relationship with the Lord. Your spiritual intimacy with each other is based on your relationship first of all to Christ and then to each other. Any other way, and your relationship becomes selfish: me, my, and mine.

The results of this selfishness are seen in many marriages. One or both persons may say, "I will stay with you as long as you make me happy. As long as things go well, as long as we have money, I will stay with you. As long as you meet my needs, I will stay." Now those of you who have gone through the agony of divorce know what I am saying. You would agree before anyone else.

When do we start teaching these concepts of intimacy to children? We start at birth and demonstrate in our own marriages to our children what a marriage should be.

Pastor, you need to preach what a marriage should be, what God intended it to be. When I pastored, I talked to my teens quite often. I would say, "All right, you lovebirds sitting back there holding hands, I want your attention." Of course I had it. "If you are planning to get married, I do not want you to plan two weeks before and then come to me and say that you have to set a date. No! I want you to start planning now."

Do not make fun of puppy love. It is real to the puppy! If young people start building unreal relationships, what they call love, and misunderstand love, they will never establish the type of relationship God has in mind for them.

So often young people start with intimacy on the physical level. Then they wonder why this physical relationship does not satisfy. They go from one physical relationship to another and never find the fulfillment they are searching for. They miss God's plan for intimacy between two people.

One night a teenage couple came into my office and told me they were in love. The fellow was very belligerent and did not want to talk in the first place. The girl was a wonderful Christian. He was not a Christian.

I said, "I want to be perfectly blunt with you, Ann. If you marry Billy, you will not be marrying a whole man. Billy is not all there."

Billy looked at me quite shocked. All of a sudden, he was interested in everything I said. I continued, "Ann, you are going to be trying to build a whole marriage and you are a Christian. You say you hope someday he will be, but he is not. He does not have the equipment to make you totally happy. Oh, a week or two, a couple of years, but he just does not have it."

Then I turned to Billy. "You see, Billy, there is a part of you that is absolutely dead. You are thinking *me, my,* and *mine* right now. You are not thinking of this girl. At this point, you two could never experience spiritual intimacy together. There would be a void in your marriage."

After the shock of his realizing his condition before God, I explained the plan of salvation to him. He trusted the Lord.

Remember, I really had been telling the truth when I had said that Billy was not a whole man. He was not all "there" until he had a spiritual dimension. When that part of his being became alive, he became a whole person. I was not calling him a half-wit; I was just not calling him a whole-wit.

So we see that two people need to have all three dimensions of intimacy balanced in a Christian marriage. Until they do, their marriage is a "hope-so" marriage and not a sure thing.

As we said at the beginning of this chapter, the times to build bridges are *times of joy*. In addition to times of birth and times of marriage, there are also:

> times of congratulations,
> times of promotions,
> times of appreciation,
> times of graduation,
> times of birthdays,
> times of anniversaries.

I remember one of my first pastorates. It was a mission. The roads were gravel and dusty and noisy. Rocks would fly. I decided the streets should be paved. We had about twelve blocks that led to the church one way and about four blocks the other. Most of the people who lived in the area were elderly.

I said, "Father, I believe we can do it." Everybody told me that I was out of my mind. And after awhile I was out of my mind trying to get everybody to sign the papers, driving hundreds of miles to find in-laws and out-laws and kinsmen to sign. It took about four or five months, but finally everybody signed. Then after all the work was done, the people were thrilled. It was really a big thing.

The construction crew supervisor who did the paving job was a big, tall man named Gus. He was very likeable. His wife would take him lunch, and my mother would send some fruit for the crew.

Finally, when the job was done, I wrote Gus a long letter of appreciation and told him what a fine job he and his crew had done and how much I appreciated it. I had not met Gus. A few days later Gus's wife stopped me in town. She yelled, "Oscar, come here."

She stood there a moment as big tears welled up in her eyes. She said, "You know Gus has been working for the city for years, and no one has ever written him a letter of appreciation." She continued, "Gus sat down the other night and read your letter over and over and just cried."

The next Sunday Gus and his wife were in church. Until this

time neither had been in church. Six weeks later I baptized both
of them.

Several months later Gus died of a heart attack. A letter—a
letter of appreciation—a letter saying you care is another way to
build bridges. Write letters of appreciation.

Birthdays

Sending birthday cards is another important way to build
bridges. A birthday is a very special day. Teachers, if you want to
build bridges to your students, this is a beautiful time to do it.
Send them birthday cards. You say, "Oh, that is time consum-
ing." I know, but it really makes a difference.

Also, think about your business associates, a business part-
ner, your business contacts, your colleagues, and employees.
Send them birthday cards. Build bridges.

When I was interim pastor at MacArthur Boulevard Baptist
Church in Irving, I sent birthday cards to every member. I sent
out many, many cards each week. My secretary at the church
would address and stamp them, but I would write a little para-
graph and sign it.

What a thrill when I stood at the back door of the church
after the service and the little children would come by and hug
my neck and give me a "moisturized" kiss that went from ear to
ear and say, "Thank you for my *birfhday* card."

Congratulations

Showing people that they are special to you is building
bridges. Suppose you want to reach teenagers. If they win district
in spelling or a football game, or if they do something special that
you read about in the newspaper, then cut the notice out of the
paper, circle it in red, and write on it, "That's great. I am proud of
you." Sign your name and send them the clipping. You will have
an open door into their world. Build bridges to these people in
your Concentric Circles.

Several of my students have come back and said, "This is

one of the most fantastic ways to reach a person whom you have not really known very well." So find out their times of joy. It is a start.

Building bridges takes time, but I do not know of anything consistently done over the years that will bear more fruit.

Times of Stress

There are many times of stress for people. An excellent time to build bridges, for example, is during sickness. You may think a person is unreachable; but in the hospital, perhaps in a critical condition, that person is open. If you want an opportunity to build a bridge, visit in the hospital. You may even meet Person X there and bring him into your circles.

If you are ever depressed and feeling sorry for yourself, go reach out to people in the hospital. They are there, and they are hurting. They need help.

Now, before you begin to make hospital visits, you need to learn how to visit sick people. So set an appointment with your pastor or other staff member or ask them for a book on how to visit people in the hospital.

The Don'ts

The first thing that you don't do is to tell a sick person how bad he looks. Don't tell him about someone with the same condition unless that person is doing well. Don't tell him how sorry you feel for him. Don't tell him about your problems. Don't share with him all the bad news you have heard. Don't stay too long.

The Do's

Do go in with a smile on your face and victory in your heart. Do share encouraging things. Do tell some good things you know that the hospitalized person would be interested in. Do stay only a short while. These are only a few things to know before visiting a patient, but they are important.

So we build bridges in times of stress: illness, surgery, death.

During times of sorrow when you reach out and love people, you have a tremendous opportunity to build bridges. Sometimes we do not know what to say at the time when someone loses a loved one. Remember, it is not as much what you say as that you care, you are concerned, you are reaching out in love. Sometimes you do not need to say anything. Your being there says enough. Remember to be attentive two or three or four weeks after a loss. Sometimes that is when the pressure really hits. That is the decision-making time. That is so often when they need a good listener.

Other times to build bridges are during:
a financial reverse,
the loss of a job,
a crisis in marriage,
a crisis with children.

Anytime you can reach out and build bridges to people in times of stress, they will never forget you.

Utilizing Points of Contact

Building bridges is a continual process. It should become a part of your life-style. The closer we are to the Lord, the more person-oriented we will become. Continually building bridges to our Immediate Family, Relatives, Close Friends, Neighbors, Business Associates, Acquaintances, and Person X's is what life is all about.

Sending a birthday card is a great way to start your life-style of bridge building, but it is only a start. The process is a continual one. We should utilize as many points of contact as possible in bridge building. Master bridge builders are what we need to become.

When you see a need, immediately begin to look for points of contact: *How do I touch this person?* If you do not have a point of contact, create one. The question is how to build bridges so that you can begin to converse with a person about things that interest him?

UTILIZING POINTS

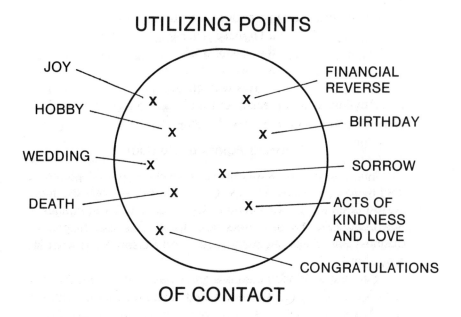

JOY

HOBBY

WEDDING

DEATH

FINANCIAL
REVERSE

BIRTHDAY

SORROW

ACTS OF
KINDNESS
AND LOVE

CONGRATULATIONS

OF CONTACT

One of my friends told me a story that happened when he was a young boy. One night he came home and saw his dad really working on something. Jim said, "Dad, what in the world are you doing?"

His dad replied, "I am working on this telegraph key, learning the Morse code."

"Why?" asked Jim. "You are not interested in ham radios."

"Yes, I am," his father replied. "You know Greg Smith's father down the street, the house with the big antenna?"

"Yes," Jim answered.

"I tried to reach him, but he would not even talk to me," Jim's dad replied. "The only thing he knows and loves is ham radio. I am going to learn how to be a ham radio operator so that I can reach Greg's dad."

Jim's dad took the time to build a bridge to Greg's dad. The bridge was a ham radio. Six months later Greg's dad trusted Jesus. That is reaching out in your Concentric Circles and building bridges.

As you meet people, begin to find out where their interests are. Then talk with them about the things that interest them.

I have a contact point with Jews because I am partially Jewish. Some time ago in Houston I met a Jewish man who was a motel desk clerk. He asked me, "Where do you work?"

I replied, "I am interim pastor at the Baptist church down the road."

"Oh," he said, "I am Jewish."

And I said, "Oh, I am too." He looked at me questioningly. I asked, "What tribe?"

"Pardon me?" he replied.

"What tribe?" I repeated.

He answered, "I am not sure. What is yours?"

I said, with quite a bit of pride, "The tribe of Judah. I will be back next weekend. Maybe you can find out this week about your tribe. We can talk more about it next week."

It is important to utilize our points of contact. As we said at the first of this chapter, we need to get on the wave lengths of those in our Concentric Circles by building bridges and establishing relationships. Building bridges to people is a continuing process.

Building Bridges in Spite of a Ruptured Relationship

As God begins to use a person, he begins to knock down walls of resistance and bad attitudes in that person's life. Some relationships in your own life, perhaps, have not been righted, and God wants to use them for his glory.

Often the first thing that comes to mind when we think of confessing a ruptured relationship is, *If I am a Christian and I admit I have been wrong in an attitude or whatever, what will the other person think of me?* Who cares what he thinks of *you.* Look at what he will think of Jesus if you do not make the relationship right.

One of my friends, Jerry Craig, was a fairly new Christian. He had a deep love for the Lord and a love to share his faith with other people. Also, he was faithful to attend services and dig into the Word. After about six months passed, he seemed to cool off. He began to lose the joy of his salvation. It troubled Jerry.

One night Jerry and his wife asked Carolyn and me over for dinner. We had a wonderful meal; then Jerry and I went off into the darkroom to work under the enlarger and to talk about things in general.

Then we sat down in the darkness with no other light on except the darkroom safe light. Jerry said, "Preacher, I have a problem. I do not know what is the matter. I have searched my heart; I have read the Word, but everything is just dry. I do not want it to be this way."

Now read very closely because someday you may be in this same state if you are not already there. It is like an airplane that quits flying. Those of you who are pilots know that when you are flying a light plane and you pull that stick back and it quits flying, the plane just settles in. You lose air speed.

Sometimes as a Christian you are going gang busters; and then all of a sudden, you just seem to settle in. You come to church, you are faithful, perhaps you even teach a Sunday School class; but you have lost the joy of your salvation.

"Well," I said, "Jerry, sometimes God wants to teach us not to depend upon emotion. God is not an emotion. Do not treat him like an emotion. Feelings come and go. Sometimes they depend on what you ate last night. Emotions fluctuate. This is caused by human physiology and human chemistry and psychological factors and the weather and who knows what else."

"No, it is more than that," Jerry replied.

"All right," I said, "let's begin to look. Is there any known sin in your life?"

"Well, I cannot think of anything," he replied. "Of course, I sin every day, but I have tried to keep short accounts with God."

I said, "Well, dear friend, I do not know exactly what is wrong; but as a babe in Christ, God will tolerate some things in your life that as you begin to mature he will not tolerate any longer. You know a mother and dad will tolerate things in a ten-month-old child that they will not tolerate when he is ten years old. Perhaps there are things in your life that God expects you to deal with at your level of maturity."

I asked, "Is there any bitterness in your life?"

"No," he said, "I am not bitter with anyone."

I said, "What about bitterness in the past?" Well, I could not have made any more impression on him if I had hit him with my fist.

He said, "Oh! Well, I had not thought about that. I have an uncle that I have hated for years. Now that I think about it, I still feel the same way."

I said, "All right, you are going to have to treat your uncle and those feelings toward your uncle just as Jesus treated you. He forgave you out of pure grace. In the same way, you are going to have to forgive your uncle. Now tell me about your uncle."

Jerry explained, "Well, when I was just a child, my father and my uncle went into business together. For a number of years the business prospered very well. Then, because it had prospered so well, my uncle pushed my father out of the business with a shrewd move. My uncle went on to become very, very wealthy. After that my father made a decent living; but it was always difficult."

Jerry continued, "Our family was angry, and I have always been angry toward my uncle."

I asked how he felt about it now. He grinned and said, "Well, let's take it to the Lord." We did.

I asked Jerry, "What now?"

Jerry replied that his attitude was right toward his uncle. I asked him if his uncle still knew that he was bitter and he replied, "Yes." I then asked him what he thought he needed to do.

"I believe I will write him," Jerry said. So Jerry wrote his uncle a letter:

DEAR UNCLE BEN,

I have had a bitterness in my heart toward you for many years. But because of a new relationship that I have with Jesus Christ, he will no longer tolerate the attitude that I have had toward you.

I want you to forgive me for my bad attitude toward you.

Now notice, he did not ask his uncle to be repentant. That was not Jerry's responsibility. Jerry's responsibility was to make his attitude right toward his uncle.

We have the tendency to say that we will ask forgiveness if the other person will. Remember, God is always the *initiator* of *reconciliation*. You show me a life where God is full and free and at liberty, and I will show you someone who is a reconciler.

Immediately, Jerry received a glowing letter back. It does not matter what the response is, however, if you have done what God asked you to do.

Jerry's uncle wrote, "Oh, Jerry, I cannot tell you how I have grieved over this misunderstanding over the years, but I have not known what to do about it. This relationship you have with Christ is very interesting."

Jerry wrote his mother and asked when Uncle Ben's birthday was. That October Jerry sent Uncle Ben a birthday card and received back another tremendous letter.

Jerry was so excited. At Christmas he sent Uncle Ben and Aunt Martha a Bible, but Jerry did not receive a word back. January passed and I asked Jerry if he had heard from Uncle Ben. He said, "No, I believe I blew it."

I will never forget that as we were preparing for a sweetheart banquet at the church on February the fourteenth, Jerry came sailing in, grabbed me, and said, "Pastor, I have to tell you something. I received a letter from Uncle Ben today." Then he handed me the letter. It said,

DEAR JERRY,
Sorry I have been so long in thanking you for the Bible, but I felt I should read it first. And you will be happy to know that after reading this Bible that I now have a relationship with Jesus Christ just like yours.

This is the key, friend: building bridges through our Concentric Circles.

Remember every time you begin to cross swords with someone, whether it is at business or home or wherever, perhaps God has engineered circumstances between you and this person in your Concentric Circles because he wants you to be a channel through which he can love and reach down and meet a person's need. People are frustrated, they are angry, they have all kinds of problems and resentments, and they need you.

I tell my students that if they are not continually bumping into people who have needs, they had better be concerned. Because if they are not continually running into unlovely people, it may mean that God has not counted them worthy to be a channel of his love. Of course, a person's deepest need is Christ. As you are building bridges, opportunities will open for you to share the gospel.

What is building bridges? It is simply meeting needs in a person's life. Just a gentle touch. Just a smile. You show me someone who intimidates people and I will show you someone who is intimidated. You show me a servant of God and I will show you someone who is *always* loving and meeting needs.

What is the purpose of a bridge? It is a structure that makes crossing over from one side to another possible. To us as Christians, building a bridge is building a relationship that lets us cross over into the world of another. Then when we have crossed over into his world, he feels safe. Then he in turn, will cross over into our world. It is a continual process. It is the process that makes a relationship.

9
Confrontation

We *must* confront people with the gospel. You say, "Well, I will just live my life before someone, but I am not good at talking." But you can talk about everything else. You talk about how to bake a cake or tell someone about football. That's no problem!

Two considerations are involved in confronting people with the gospel by just living your life before them. Number one, you are going to have to live a better life than Jesus did because he not only lived the gospel but he talked about it also. Two, if you live a good life and no one knows the source of the power in your life, you have lost the battle.

Don't Browbeat People

Sharing the gospel or sharing what Jesus has done in your life should not be a problem. You say, "But I am afraid." I know you are, but do not be afraid. When you begin to pray for people and to love them and meet their needs, the Lord will prepare their hearts; he will prepare yours also. Just simply talk to people about what the Lord means in your life, share John 3:16, or whatever. Then when God does his mighty work in their hearts, they are ready. Do not browbeat people. Just talk to them naturally, in love. Do not be afraid. But if you are afraid, let's think about the *worst* thing that could happen to you. This story may help you to decide.

Years ago I took five of my laymen to a crusade in California. We were assigned to Reno, Nevada, which is a part of the California Convention; and we had a marvelous time.

The men who came for us at the air terminal began to prepare us for the crusade immediately.

Some Say It Is Difficult to Share

"Now, brethren, you are not in the Bible Belt," they warned us. "It is hard to witness out here." By the time we reached the general meeting, they had told us five times how difficult it was to witness in Reno. This really built our confidence.

My five laymen were successful businessmen and knew about the ways of the world. But they were also men who had a great love for God and loved to share him with other people.

When we arrived at the meeting, each of us were asked to say a word; but before we did, we were reminded again about how hard it was to witness in Reno. We knew these people needed encouragement.

The Worst Possible Thing

One of my laymen stood up and said lovingly, "Brethren, we have heard that it is difficult to witness here. I understand that. I am thankful for the work that is going on here. But I want to ask you something. What is the worst possible thing they could do to you?"

There was silence. Then one little boy on the front row stood up and yelled, "Kill ya!"

"How many have you lost lately?" my layman asked. Everyone laughed and relaxed.

What the Preacher Was Taught

Those five fellows taught me many things that week. They said, "If we have good news to tell, we are going to tell it to anybody who will listen to us." God works when we make ourselves available.

One afternoon three of the men were with me driving to the laundromat to do our laundry. All of a sudden one of the fellows said, "Stop!"

"Why?" I asked, slamming on the brakes.

"There is a lady watering her yard," one answered. "Let's talk to her."

Like paratroopers, all three piled out of the car and encountered this woman in her yard. I stayed in the car. They talked for awhile. Then she turned off the water, and they all started toward the house. They motioned for me to come.

I thought to myself, *You're nuts, I have taught you better than to go into a house with a woman by yourselves.* Two teenagers appeared at the door. I was delighted that someone else was home.

I thought, *Oh, boy. Here goes nothing.* I got out of the car, went into the house, and introduced myself. Then I sat down and waited to see what would happen next.

The lady said, "I am so glad you have come. My husband and I separated last week, and it has been torment. My two teenagers have been so upset. We do not belong to a church, and we really have had no one to talk to."

So the fellows shared the gospel. It was a very simple presentation, but it met needs. The woman said, "Oh, I never understood all of that before. You know, I have been so depressed. I was just out there watering my roses, asking God, if there was a God, 'Can you help me?' Then you walked up."

The mother and two teenagers accepted Christ right there. She said they would be at the services that evening.

God was engineering circumstances. God was preparing hearts. But someone had to be available, and someone had to confront.

One-arm Bandits in a Grocery Store

At this same time two other of my laymen had gone to the store for groceries. Now one of those fellows could sell ice to the Eskimos.

As the two entered the grocery store, they noticed a fellow sticking money into a "one-arm bandit." In Reno, slot machines are in every grocery store.

One layman walked over to the fellow at the slot machine and said, "That won't pay off!" (These men did not get all of their techniques from me.)

The layman continued, "Seriously, you are wasting your money. I have something that will really pay off!"

"What?" the fellow asked.

My layman said, "Well, let's talk." So all three went outside the store and stood by the car. The layman led the man to the Lord.

As we ate before the service, we all rejoiced over the people who had come to know the Lord that afternoon.

Meeting at the Altar

About two hundred people attended the evening service. It was a glorious service. When I gave the invitation, the man from the grocery store came down one aisle and the mother and two teenagers came down the other. They saw each other at the altar. The couple that was separated was reunited in the Lord.

Talk about the Holy Spirit's engineering circumstances! Humanly, how could this problem have been solved? God is in the business of answering prayer. He specializes in it. We make ourselves available by praying: "Father, here I am. Make me a channel to meet the needs of those around me."

Do We Really Love Him?

Our love for God must precede our love for the lost. If we really love *him,* we will *love* whom *he* loves. We must realize man's lost condition without God. If we *believe* the *Word,* then we do not have any option. When the Scriptures say a person is *lost* without the Lord, that is exactly what they mean. You can bring all the theological speculation to bear that you want. The fact still is that a person without Christ is lost. Often we have tried to water down the gospel, to make it unrejectable. But the thread runs all the way through the Bible: "No one comes to the Father, but through me." (John 14:6). "There is no other name under heaven that has been given among men, by which we must be saved" (Acts. 4:12). "He who has the Son has the life; he who does not have the Son of God does not have the life" (1 John 5:12).

If it did not take the *death* of Jesus Christ to *redeem* man, then the *cross* was a *travesty*. It was useless. No! He had to come and die. There was *no other way*. If he is the *only* way, then men are *lost* without him. We need to weep over that. A person cannot be changed until he realizes, "Without Christ, I am *hopelessly* and *helplessly lost."*

When you begin to think about a mom or dad or child or loved one in Circle 2 or Circle 3, when you think of Close Friends in Circle 4, or Neighbors or Business Associates in Circle 5, Acquaintances in Circle 6, and Person X in Circle 7, remember, if they are *without* Christ, they are *lost*. You need to be concerned about their lostness. We do not know how long any of us have. You need to see the urgency.

Jesus said, "What will a man be profited, if he gains the whole world, and forfeits his soul?" (Matt. 16:26). Soul means the totality of the person.

Seeing People as God Sees Them

The *closer* you get to God, the more you *value* human life. I will never forget the first day the nurses brought our baby girl to the window for me to see. I looked down and she looked up, and I knew she was thinking, *That's my daddy*. Human life. How precious it is.

One of my colleagues said, "You know, Oscar, I was sitting in the airport in Los Angeles the other day. You can see just about anything and everything in an airport. I was watching people walk and noticing their different clothes, their different smells, and their different looks, and I found myself judging them. Why are they like that? All of a sudden it dawned on me. I got that nudge from the Lord, 'Careful, my child, I made them.' All of a sudden I began to see people as *God sees them:* precious, infinitely precious."

When you talk to someone in one of your inner circles, or your outer circles, perhaps your Circle 7—the person in the grocery store, at the service station, in the jail, or at a restaurant, remember, *God made him.* He *loves* him. He wants you to be sensitive to his needs, to care about him.

Rejecting "Churchianity"

Remember, many people do not reject Christ; they reject a caricature of him. They never really hear the message. How many of you at one time or another rejected a caricature of the Lord? You were rejecting a concept of "churchianity" as you saw it. You were never really confronted with the claims of the person of Jesus Christ and what you needed to do to have fellowship with him.

When you look at any lost person, remember that person has the *ability* to have *fellowship* with the God of this universe. We need to think about that.

Who Is Your God?

Have we forgotten who our God is? The very immensity and power of this Sovereign Being is hard for us to comprehend. "Father, help me if you can!" we sometimes say.

The psalmist spent much time talking about the stars, the moon, the sun, and the many other handiworks of God because he realized who God is and what he created.

Light travels at the speed of about 186,000 miles per second. One little boy said, "Man, that will outrun a Chevrolet." Multiply that by sixty and you have one light hour. Multiple that by twenty-four and you have one light day, and then multiply that by three hundred and sixty-five and you have one light year. Light travels about six trillion miles in one light year.

Our nearest star is Alpha Centauri. We cannot see it because it is in the southern hemisphere. However, if you could see Alpha Centauri tonight, you might say, "Look at Alpha Centauri." Actually you would be seeing the light that left Alpha

Centauri four and one-third light years ago. That is our *nearest* star.

Until early in the twentieth century, astronomers thought that the Milky Way was the only galaxy in the universe. It has a diameter of about 100 thousand light years. They tell us now that there are billions of galaxies. And the One who put everything together, we call Father. But we can only call him Father through Jesus Christ.

Just think, a little finite being created in the image of the God of this universe has the ability to have fellowship with that God every day. For us to neglect to tell people how they can know God is unthinkable.

One night years ago, as I was preaching about these wonders of God that the psalmist talked about, I said, "When God rolls back eternity, Buster, where are you going to be when the 'big show' starts?" Of course, I had no particular person in mind. But during the invitation, a twenty-year-old fellow, tears streaming down his cheeks, came forward. He said, "I'm Buster, and I need to trust Jesus." That is what you call "calling them out."

Do you know the reason the cults and sects are pulling our young people into their groups? It is because the cults find a lonely, troubled, perhaps disillusioned, empty youngster who is not being reached and loved. They say, "We will take care of you. We will love you." The young person is drawn in. We must confront such young people in our Concentric Circles.

Confrontation Now

A time should come when we confront people in our Concentric Circles. We need to say, "Has there ever come a time in your life when you have come to know Jesus Christ in a personal way, or would you say you are still in the process?" Sometimes we pray and pray. But when God nudges us, when he says it is time to confront them, we are silent.

One day I walked into the bookstore at the seminary. One of my students grabbed me and said: "Dr. Thompson, I have to conduct a funeral for a lost person; and I desperately need some help. I have never done this before; I am really troubled about it."

I said, "Well, I understand. I will be in my office in about thirty minutes. Come on up, and we will work on it together."

So he came to my office, and we sat down. I said, "I know it is difficult. I have had to conduct funerals for lost people too many times. Who is it?"

"My uncle," he replied.

I said, "Now, let's see, how much time do we have? When is the funeral?"

"I do not know," he replied.

I thought, *Well, the arrangements have not been made yet,* so I said, "Will it be in a couple of days?"

"Oh, no, not necessarily," he answered.

I thought, *Boy, they are going to mummify this guy before they bury him.* I did not tell him that. It would not have been an appropriate thing to say.

So trying very hard to keep my composure, I asked, "What do you mean?"

"He is not dead yet, Dr. Thompson," the fellow replied.

"But you told me it was a funeral for a lost person!"

"Well, he is, but I do not believe he is going to be saved," he said. "People have been praying for him for years. He is an intellectual and just not reachable. Now he has developed emphysema, and his lungs are collapsing."

"I'll tell you what," I said. "I have a better idea. Let's claim Matthew 18:19 for your uncle. Our Lord said, 'If two of you agree on earth about anything that they may ask, it shall be done for them by My Father who is in heaven.' "

"Let's stand between this man and hell and ask God to save him. His problem is not knowledge. His problem is conviction. He needs to realize that he is lost. You cannot convict him. That is the Holy Spirit's job. So let's ask God to engineer circumstances to bring your uncle to Christ."

After we had prayed, I asked, "Has anyone ever confronted him?"

"Well, yes. People have asked him to come to church."

"No," I said, "that is not what I am talking about. Has anyone ever sat down and said, 'Dear friend, I want to tell you the best news that I have ever heard,' and just shared with him who Jesus is and what Jesus did and what it should mean to him. Has he ever been confronted with those three things: his present need, Christ's provision, and an appeal for him to accept what has been done for him?"

"Well," he said. "I do not know if he would listen to me."

I said, "Dear friend, isn't that his decision? What does he have to gain if he does and what does he have to lose if he does not. He needs to be able to make the choice."

Several weeks later I saw that student in the hall. He said, "Dr. Thompson, my uncle has been saved. It was the first time I had ever shared the gospel, and he was saved. When I confronted him with the simple truth, do you know what he said?"

I said, "No."

"My uncle said, 'You know I never could buy all of this religion bit because people would never tell me what they were talking about, and I was too proud to ask.' "

That's it. Just talk to people in a normal voice and tell them what Jesus has done for you and can do for them. Confront them with who Jesus is, what sin is, and how God has provided for forgiveness of sin.

As a great, old, Methodist preacher once said, "I heard the gospel, and I heard the gospel, and I heard the gospel, and then one day, praise God, I heard the gospel."

A person has to be convicted by the Holy Spirit; he has to realize that he is lost before he can be saved. He has to see himself as he is in God's sight. When a person stands morally naked before God, he sees himself as God sees him. This is what the Holy Spirit of God does through the Word and in answer to intercessory prayer. This is confrontation.

10
The Real Purpose of Life

When we look at life—and the last few years I have had many opportunities to look at the length as well as the brevity of life with many people—I think we need to pinpoint our priorities. Too much of our lives, too much of our ministries, are frittered away on nonessentials. If we are to do what God calls us to do in the time that he has given us to do it, we must know our priorities, zero in on them, and accomplish them. Jesus sets the priority.

We all need checklists to accomplish things correctly. I remember what my flight instructor said to me when I was first learning to fly: "This is your checklist. You are a young pilot, but if you want to live to be an old pilot, you will always use your checklist."

For the Christian, I feel John 15:1-12 is a checklist. I have found that when I feel out of touch, out of focus, out of sorts, I should go back to my checklist. It reads:

I AM the true vine, and My Father is the vinedresser. Every branch in Me that does not bear fruit, He takes away; and every *branch* that bears fruit, He prunes it, that it may bear more fruit. You are already clean because of the word which I have spoken to you. Abide in Me, and I in you. As the branch cannot bear fruit of itself, unless it abides in the vine, so neither *can* you, unless you abide in Me. I am the vine, you are the branches; he who abides in Me, and I in him, he bears much fruit; for apart from Me you can do nothing. If anyone does not abide in Me, he is thrown away as a branch, and dries up; and they gather them, and cast them into the fire, and they are burned. If you abide in Me, and My words abide in you, ask whatever you wish, and it shall be done for you. By this is My Father glorified, that you bear much fruit, and *so* prove to be My disciples. Just as the Father has loved Me, I have also loved you; abide in My love. If you keep My commandments, you will abide in My love; just as I have kept My Father's commandments, and abide in His love. These things I have spoken to you, that My joy may be in you, and *that* your joy may be made full. This is My commandment, that you love one another, just as I have loved you.

The Purpose for Our Existence

Pastors, remember that your church has not only received you as a person *per se* but it has also received a life. That life preaches through the Word of God. The Word is to be real in your life. What you preach should not come from a theory, but it should flow out of a life that is in agreement with the living God.

Now the purpose for your occupying space and taking up oxygen, your reason for existence, is to bear fruit. If you are not bearing fruit, there is no reason for your existence.

The Word says that if you want to glorify the Father, you will bear fruit. If you want to demonstrate that you are his disciple, you will bear fruit. If you want to be a blessing to the world, you will bear fruit.

This is such an important parable for every Christian to understand. I want you to understand that I believe in John 15 Jesus was *not* talking about being saved or lost. He was talking about a Christian's bearing fruit. Jesus used fruit bearing because the people knew what he was talking about. He was reaching into their world so that he could communicate with them.

Today in our economy and in our way of life, we do not understand much about vines. But in that day, the people understood perfectly; so we have to translate both the idea of the fruit and the idea that Jesus is conveying.

What is Fruit?

Now you may ask, "What is fruit? Is it service for the Lord?" No.

"Is it attending services or praying?" No.

"Is it souls we have won?" No.

"Is it buildings, baptisms, or budgets?" No.

These things overflow out of fruit, but they are not what we are talking about when we say "bearing fruit."

Fruit always comes from the *nature* of the *seed*. Whatever the nature of the seed will also be the nature of the fruit. If you plant a peach pit, you will get a peach tree. If you plant a plum seed, you will get a plum tree. A watermelon seed produces watermelon vines. And I suppose if there were a spaghetti seed and you planted it, you would get a spaghetti plant.

Fruit comes from the nature of the seed, and the seed is the Word of God. It is God's Person and his written Word. "In the beginning was the Word, and the Word was with God, and the Word was God. . . . All things came into being through Him; and apart from Him nothing came into being that has come into being" (John 1:1,3).

The Word of God tells us that God wants to produce his character in our lives. So to bear fruit means that we allow the character of God to be produced in our lives.

Galatians 5:22-23 says that the *fruit* of the Spirit is:

Love—the relationship
Joy—the result of the relationship
Peace—the result of the correct relationship
Long-suffering (patience)—the maintenance of the relationship
Gentleness—the attitude of the relationship
Goodness—the outgoing blessing of the relationship
Faith—the means of the relationship
Meekness—the submitted will in the relationship
Self-Control—the control of the relationship

So the nature of the seed, the nature of the Word, the nature of God will be reproduced in the life of the believer. If that does *not* happen, there is a major problem in the life of the believer.

The fruit is the very character of God. Jesus came to earth;

he lived his life. What he saw his Father do is what he did. What
he heard his Father say is what he said (John 14:10-11). Jesus
was in total submission to the Father. As a result of that submission, the Father manifested his character in Jesus. Jesus came to
earth not only to die for us but also to manifest the character of
the Father so that people can see what God is like.

I have a beautiful martin house on a little hill out in my backyard. It is for purple martins, birds who eat their weight in
mosquitoes and other pesky insects each day. It is on a telescop-
ing pole. Several months ago when I was out of town, one of the
nuts on the pole slipped; the martin house dropped down. When
I got back home, I found it about four feet off the ground.

Now, the martins did not seem bothered too much, but I
was afraid the cats would get to them. So I went out to raise it. Of
course, I was staring the birds right in the face. They scattered
like a covey of quail and really fussed at me. I ran the pole all the
way up and secured it.

But one old bird in that group decided I had done something
terribly wrong. Now every time I walk out into the backyard, she
flies to about sixty feet and dives at me, coming about twelve
inches from my head. Then, just as she passes my head, she
goes "chirrup!" She does not bother Damaris; she does not
bother our puppies, Burfaldine or Neigette; she does not bother
Carolyn; she does not bother our guests. Just me!

I was standing out in the backyard several days later when I
said to her, "You dummy, don't you know I was lifting your
house back up so a cat, skunk, or whatever could not bother
your babies?" But she, like some fighter plane coming out of a
cloud, just dived down and buzzed right over my head. I said, "I
wish I could communicate with you, but I cannot. I do not know
bird language." I tried it. I went "chirrup," but she just kept
coming back.

Do you see the point? God said, "I want to communicate
with people." Jesus Christ entered history. John 1:14 says that
Jesus is the Word. God sent Jesus to build a bridge to people, to

be able to communicate with them, to be able to develop a relationship with them. Jesus is the One who reveals the character of the Father. Isn't that beautiful? Jesus built the bridge between God and people so that we can have a relationship with God.

Bearing fruit is the nature of Jesus. I once heard someone ask a black man, "What is a Christian?"

He smiled and replied, "Just Jesus running around in a black body." Or a white one, or a red one, or a yellow one, or whatever else.

Bearing fruit is Jesus Christ manifesting his character in our lives, Jesus' life-style in us. Listen carefully. Jesus wants his life-style to be manifested in your life.

Remember, Paul said that God has given to us two things: the Word of reconciliation and the ministry of reconciliation (2 Cor. 5:18-19). Our lives are to be linked with God since God by his grace and by the cross linked us with himself. Then he gives us that ability to reach out and build bridges to a lost world. That is what life is all about. This is bearing fruit.

When your life is bearing his fruit, you are bearing his life. You do not produce the fruit, he does. You bear it.

Jesus said, "I am the vine, you are the branches"; (John 15:5). In other words, you are a glorified grape rack. All you can do is bear the fruit. You cannot produce it. The vine, which is Jesus, produces it. Have you ever seen a tree saying, "Oh, I just have to produce some fruit"? No. It just does what it is designed to do.

The Results of Bearing Fruit

Three passages in John 15 tell about the results of bearing fruit. Let's give them direction.

Upward Reach

First is the *upward* reach. Jesus said, "If you abide in Me, and My words abide in you, ask whatever you wish, and it shall be done for you" (John 15:7). A person who has fellowship and a close walk with the Lord Jesus Christ is going to live in a spirit and life-style of answered prayer. When he prays, things happen. One of the greatest marks of a Christian's life is that he has answered prayer.

I ask you, Is God answering prayer in your life? Well, he cannot answer prayer unless you are praying. "You do not have because you do not ask" (Jas. 4:2). You will not bear much fruit if you are not spending time as an intercessor. I believe the greatest battle in evangelism is at this point. The greatest battle in living for Jesus is at this point.

In fellowship with Jesus, knowing that I am dependent on the Father for everything, I come to him, spend time with him, and talk to him. Then his Holy Spirit reveals things in and through my life. It is of divine necessity that the believer be a great talker with God.

Inward Joy

The second result of bearing fruit is *inward joy*. John 15:11 says, "These things I have spoken to you, that My joy may be in you."

If you will study the Beatitudes, you will notice that Jesus uses the word, "blessed," which comes from the Greek word *makarios*. This was the word used for the Isle of Cyprus meaning that if a person lived in Cyprus, he had everything that he could possibly need within the confines of that island. It was a blessed state. There was a sense of satisfaction, a sense of fulfillment. There was a sense of joy in that blessedness.

Dear friend, if you are walking in Jesus Christ and have found him sufficient, your life is filled with a sense of blessedness. That is *inward* joy.

I am not talking about outward circumstances. Outward circumstances may be terrible. Do not depend on happenings to make you happy. If things happen happy, you are happy. If they do not happen happy, you are not happy. NO! If you live like this, your life will *never* be tranquil.

No matter what the outward circumstances are, joy is an inward relationship with God that gives peace and joy. Do you have inward joy? If you are bearing fruit, you will have inward joy.

Joy comes from a relationship. Remember that the most important word in the English language is *relationship*. A relationship with Jesus Christ brings joy. That relationship with him will determine our relationships with others.

Outward *Agape* Love

The third result of bearing fruit is *outward agape love. Love is meeting needs.* This kind of love comes from his resources, not ours. We are going to bear it. We cannot produce it, only he can. We are only the channel of his love. God has never told us he loved us without meeting our needs. "God so loved the world, that He *gave*. . . ." (John 3:16, author's italics).

"God demonstrates His own *love* toward us, in that while we were yet sinners, Christ *died* for us" (Rom. 5:8, author's italics).

"We know [the] love [of God] by this, that He laid down His *life* for us" (1 John 3:16, author's italics).

"But God, being rich in mercy, because of His great *love* with which He loved us, even when we were dead in our transgressions, made us *alive*" (Eph. 2:4-5, author's italics).

Every time you find God loving us he is meeting our needs. Loving people is meeting needs. Loving may not be a feeling. Although *philia* love is tied to feelings, *agape* love does not depend on feelings. It is a commitment of the will saying, "I am going to meet those needs out of the resources of God." The feeling may follow; it may not. But the real essence of the love that Jesus spoke about—the love that will flow through us—is best illustrated when he talked about how God loves.

Do you remember the story of the two farmers in chapter 6? One loved the Lord and the other abhorred him. But the Scriptures say that God made the sun to shine and the rain to fall on them both (Matt. 5:45). There are no favorites with God.

You may say, "I am going to love the lost. I am going to love that person out there." No, dear friend, unless you are loving everybody in your circles, loving without discrimination, your love may not be flowing from the Holy Spirit. It may be a I-love-me-and-I-want-you-to-make-me-happy kind of love.

Now if I do not love (meet the needs) my daughter, Damaris, and my wife, Carolyn, and love those in my inner circle, then I am not loving as I should.

Love for Jesus means I love everybody in sight. I love those for whom God has given me responsibility. It is my responsibility to meet the needs of Carolyn, whatever those needs are, and to meet the needs of Damaris.

As God brings people into my life, whoever they are, he brings them there for a purpose. God then says, "Now, Oscar, you meet their needs, not out of your resources, but out of mine." I become a channel for meeting needs. This is what Jesus was saying. If we are bearing fruit, we will be loving without discrimination.

And do you know what? If we can get our churches to see that we are to love without discrimination and that we are to give the Holy Spirit liberty to love everybody in sight through our churches, then we would have revival on our hands. The world would turn aside to see the "burning bush."

Hindrances to Bearing Fruit

All this discussion of bearing fruit may raise a question in your mind: Why am I not bearing fruit? Jesus revealed three hindrances to bearing fruit:

Behold, the sower went out to sow; and as he sowed, some *seeds* fell beside the road, and the birds came and devoured them. And others fell upon the rocky places, where they did not have much soil; and immediately they sprang up, because they had no depth of soil. But when the sun had risen, they were scorched; and because they had no root, they withered away. And others fell among the thorns, and the thorns came up and choked them out. And others fell on the good soil, and yielded a crop, some a hundredfold, some sixty, and some thirty (Matt. 13:3-8).

In six short verses, Jesus presented the parable involving the stolen, the shallow, the choked, and the good seed.

Parable of the Sower	Jesus' Explanation
Stolen Seed Matthew 13:4	Matthew 13:19
Shallow Seed Matthew 13:5-6	Matthew 13:20-21
Choked Seed Matthew 13:7	Matthew 13:22
Good Seed Matthew 13:8	Matthew 13:23

The Stolen Seed

Jesus said: "Hear then the parable of the sower. When any one hears the word of the kingdom, and does not understand it, the evil *one* comes and snatches away what has been sown in his heart. This is the one on whom seed was sown beside the road" (Matt. 13:18-19).

Jesus said the sower went forth to sow. What happened? The sower sowed the seed and the "evil one" came and stole the seed.

I want to ask you what your preacher preached on last Sunday? What was taught in your Sunday School class? Listen very closely. The *key* in fruit bearing is the germination of the seed. It makes no difference how much seed is sown; if the seed does not germinate, it does not bear fruit.

Satan is not concerned with how many people gather in a service if all they do is sit and listen and leave. Satan does not care how much seed is sown as long as he can *steal it* away.

There needs to be an encounter with the living God and an encounter with his Word. The seed of the Word of God needs to be dropped into people's hearts and then germinated by faith. Then the Holy Spirit takes it and produces new life. The tragedy is that many people go to the services, fill the Sunday School classes, are counted in attendance, but then slip away. Their lives are no different; they bear no fruit; they do not touch the world; they are not reconciling the world to Christ.

Now, at this point we must assume two things. The parable of the sower assumes that the *seed has been sown.* It is a big assumption for our day, is it not? Many times there is no seed sown. Preacher, do not tell people what you think. Instead tell them what the Word of God says. Open the Scriptures and make them live for your people. If no seed is sown, there will be no germination.

I receive letters and telephone calls from people all over the country who say, "We need a preacher who will preach the Word." Now this means that we need men who are able to take the Scriptures and, in the power of the Holy Spirit, present them in such a way that they become alive, where people can understand and say, "I received a word from the Lord."

It is also the responsibility of the Sunday School teachers to make sure the Word of God has been shared in their classes. We must teach the Word of God. This mighty burden is on the pastor, on every Sunday School teacher, and on each proclaimer of the Word. Whatever your status, God holds *you* responsible for making sure that the people in your Concentric Circles know what God's Word says.

But in Matthew 13:19 we have read that it is not enough that the Word of God be sown because there is a supernatural power afoot to snatch the Word of God away from us. Satan does not mind how much you have been under the sound of the Word if that Word does not fall into your heart and germinate and bring forth fruit.

Distraction from the Word of God is one of the greatest problems that we have in the world today. If a pastor would be so bold as to stand at the back door and ask, "What did I preach this morning?" how many would remember?

A second problem is that, though you may preach a masterful message, pastor, if the people in your congregation do not realize that the Word of God is to be meditated upon, it will not

bear fruit. *Meditation* is taking the Word of God and covering it
by faith, so that it germinates like a seed, springs forth, and bears
fruit.

But so often the tragedy is that the Word is stolen away. Do
people carry the Word of God out with them from our Sunday
School classes or from our preaching services? Is the Word of
God planted firmly so that God can encounter the human personality and the human soul? Whenever we try to remember a
Scripture passage, a supernatural power will be afoot to steal it
away.

The Shallow Seed

Let's look at Matthew 13:20-21. "The one on whom seed
was sown on the rocky places, this is the man who hears the
word, and immediately receives it with joy; yet he has no *firm*
root in himself, but is *only* temporary, and when affliction or
persecution arises because of the word, immediately he falls
away."

Have you ever been in a service and heard a sermon that
you felt the Lord sent just for you? It met your particular need—
encouragement, correction, insight, or whatever. You are convicted and the Word germinates. It takes hold.

Let me give you a spiritual principle: The moment the Word
germinates and takes hold the processes of nature take hold to
see if the seed is going to bear fruit.

Let me explain. The sun comes out. Now isn't that what
Jesus said in verse 6? The sun comes out and will test that seed.
Is the sun there to destroy the seed? No. The sun is there to help
that seed produce luxurious fruit. But the same sun that *produces* luxurious fruit in one seed *scorches* another plant, and it
withers. In other words, the testing is *not* to *destroy* the fruit; it is
to *produce* it.

Have you ever seen this happen? A set of circumstances
moves into one believer's life and he remains or abides in Christ,

soaks up the strength of the vine, takes the life of the vine, and produces the character of Christ.

Another person, under the same set of circumstances, does not abide in the vine as he should. He knows the principles; but instead of bearing fruit, he becomes bitter and hard and angry with God. He says, "Why has this happened to me? Why has this come?" His fruit withers and dies.

Has that ever happened to you? You see, God always takes his children and places them in circumstances that have potential for bearing fruit. How we react by faith determines the fruit. For example, you hear a sermon on "Love your neighbor." You really should love your neighbor, shouldn't you? The Scripture says that you are to love your neighbor. So you say, "I am going to love my neighbor."

You talk on the way home about how you are going to love your neighbors. You think about ways to give them attention. You are so happy. You get home and guess who is standing in your driveway? One of your neighbors. He indignantly says, "Your dog just dug up all my daffodils!" *The sun is out.* Are you going to *wither* or *bear* fruit? Here is your opportunity. You see, any old pharisee can love folk who love him. It does not take any of God's grace to love those who love you. But it takes God's supernatural grace to love those who do not love you.

The point is that after you receive a fresh, new insight into the Word of God, the Lord will allow that truth to be tested in your life. He will show you that he is adequate for *any* circumstance, just as his Word says he is. He wants you to bear fruit.

Every circumstance that comes into your life is an opportunity for God to demonstrate his power in your life. The heat comes—the heat of circumstances, the heat of persecution, the heat of wrong feelings. These crises come into your life. All of the circumstances swirl about you and you think, *Lord, what happened?* Nothing. God is just producing fruit in your life.

How many times have you wilted? How many times has God put you in a circumstance? You got an insight from his

Word. You received it with joy. Then there came a test, and you blew it?

If, as you begin to pray through your Concentric Circles, all hell breaks loose, do not be alarmed. If when you share with someone they chew you up one side and down the other, God just wants to demonstrate his love and gentleness in return by your turning the other cheek (Matt. 5:39). Most people have never understood that passage. God wants to demonstrate his character in your life.

The Choked Seed

"The one on whom seed was sown among the thorns, this is the man who hears the word, and the worry of the world, and the deceitfulness of riches choke the word, and it becomes unfruitful" (Matt. 13:22).

Does this seed germinate? Yes. Was it growing into a fine plant? Yes. But all of a sudden other things choked it out. Did it bear fruit? No. Something choked it. What chokes us? The number one problem we have is worry, little anxieties. You cannot praise God and worry at the same time. The word translated "worry" in verse 22 is *merimna*. This is a Greek word that runs through the Scriptures. It is used in Matthew 6:31, "Do not be anxious"; in 1 Peter 5:7, "Casting all your anxiety upon Him"; and in Philippians 4:6, "Be anxious for nothing."

With the negative as used in these verses, *merimna* means not to let anxiety eat at you. You are not to let it grasp you. If you leave a garden hoe out in the morning dew for several days, you will find that it has begun to rust. This is oxidation, and it has eaten into the hoe. This is the meaning of *merimna*. God is telling us not to let the corrosive care of this world eat on us.

Are you anxious about business, about a child, about your marriage, or about many things? Then weeds are choking the seed, and you will not bear fruit.

One lady came to me and asked, "But Brother Oscar, why pray when I can worry?" Listen, friend, God gives us grace for one day at a time. Do not let the worries of tomorrow choke out the peace and joy of today. Worry will choke out the fruit. Remember that Jesus is our inheritance and that he will never allow anything to enter into our lives that he will not supply the grace and strength for us to bear it.

I remember going to a new church in my younger days as a pastor and having a deacon try to intimidate me. He said, "Unless you fire that educational director . . ." But I do not fire educational directors, and I do not hire them. They come from the Lord.

This deacon said, "Unless you fire him, several families will leave the church."

I sort of grinned and put my arm around him and asked, "What are you trying to tell me?"

He answered, "Well, we will lose their tithes and that might hurt your salary." Hear that old squeeze? I had been there only three weeks.

So I just hugged him real tight and said, "Let me tell you a secret."

"What is it?" he asked.

"I am independently wealthy," I whispered.

"You are?" he said.

I explained, "You see, my Father owns the cattle on a thousand hills. He sets my salary."

That man became my dearest friend. We did not lose one person, and I surely did not fire that good man who was trying to carry on a ministry that the church was too hardhearted to recognize.

Do not be intimidated when you are walking in the Spirit. Christ is your inheritance, and he may very well put you in a place where you have to choose between the deceitfulness of riches or bearing fruit. The deceitfulness of riches will choke out the seed because it promises to pay off, and it cannot. The things that really satisfy the deepest longings of a person's heart are not the things in your hands that you possess, but relationships.

Bearing Fruit

"The one on whom seed was sown on the good ground, this is the man who hears the word and understands it; who indeed bears fruit, and brings forth, some a hundredfold, some sixty, and some thirty" (Matt. 13:23).

This person bears much fruit. What is the result of being filled with the Spirit? As we have listed earlier in this chapter, Christ's character is the fruit of the Spirit as seen in Galatians 5:22-23.

If you are bearing fruit, remember these three directions: upward, inward, and outward. Remember also that God will never let anything come into your life except by his permission. If it comes with his permission, it comes with his grace and strength. But he gives that grace for one day at a time. What is your purpose for occupying space and taking up oxygen? What is your purpose for living? To bear fruit. If you do not bear fruit, then someday when you stand before him, your hands will be empty.

11
Disciple

Someday all Christians will give an account of their lives to the Lord. He has given us many commandments by which we are to live. His last commandment, often called the Great Commission, is found in Matthew 28:19-20: "Go therefore and make disciples of all nations, baptizing them in the name of the Father and the Son and the Holy Spirit, teaching them to observe all that I commanded you; and lo, I am with you always, even unto the end of the age."

In these verses, the word that seems to carry the most emphasis is the word "Go." However, this is not true in the Greek. The only Greek imperative in this passage is the word *matheteusate* which is a second person plural, first aorist active imperative. The word *matheteusate* is derived from the Greek root word *mathetes* which means "disciple." The other three words, Going . . . baptizing . . . teaching, all participles, derive their force from the imperative, "make disciples." So these two verses in Greek may be translated, "Therefore, as you are going, disciple all nations, baptizing them in the name of the Father and the Son and the Holy Spirit, teaching them to observe all things whatsoever I gave command to you; and behold I am with you all the days until the completion of the age."

We are good at teaching, and we are good at baptizing. But somehow we have lost our central theme. We are not very good at making disciples as we are going.

First let's clarify several things about these verses of Scripture called the Great Commission. Jesus assumed that we were *going.* He used a participle, "as you are going," so it is understood that we are going. However, I am afraid that often we have had a reversal of the Great Commission. So often we, as the followers of Jesus, say, "Come and hear" rather than, "As you are going, tell."

Every time I ask my students what the word *disciple* means, I get five dozen different answers. What does *disciple* mean? It will be very difficult to go out and make disciples if we do not have a clear concept of what a disciple is.

One of the most important terms for a learner in the New Testament is from *manthanein* which means "to learn." The word for disciple *(mathetes)* is derived from *manthanein,* meaning that a disciple is a learner. Damaris goes to school to *manthano* (I learn or I am taught). It is a teaching relationship between Damaris and her teachers. Next year Damaris will not have the same teachers. The students come and sit in class and learn, then they move on to other teachers.

Most of the teaching in the Jewish world was done in the home and in the scribal schools. In the Greek world, however, it was often done by what we would call *peripatetic* teachers. (*peri* means around—*pateo* means to walk) The teachers walked from place to place, teaching their particular philosophy. In each place, they gathered a class, taught, extracted a fee for their time, and went on their way. The relationship between teacher and student was much as it is in our day and time. It was simply a relationship of learning.

As already indicated, the word used in the Great Commission is from the Greek word *mathetes,* disciple. The word *mathetes* embodies several characteristics of a genuine disciple. In this chapter we will discuss four of them.

(1) A disciple has a personal relationship with the teacher.
(2) A disciple is under the total authority of the teacher.
(3) A disciple possesses and demonstrates the character of the teacher.
(4) A disciple must be prepared to suffer for the teacher.

A Disciple Has a Personal Relationship with the Teacher

You cannot become a disciple through a correspondence course. A disciple has a personal relationship with the teacher. Can you have a personal relationship with Buddha? Muhammed? Moon? No! Only a handful could. But the reason that Jesus went away and the Holy Spirit came was so that he could actually reside in you.

You should not have to go back to a time twenty years ago when you were saved or look in a baptismal record to see if you have been born again. That is poor discipleship. There needs to be a time when today—not yesterday, not last week—you have fellowship with the living God.

I am reminded of the story of a testimony meeting years ago. One woman stood up and sarcastically said, "Well, God saved me forty years ago. My cup has neither gone dry nor has it run over." Then she sat down.

One little boy nudged another little boy on the front row and said, "Yeah, and I bet her cup has wiggle tails in it, too." Do not let that happen to you.

Let me remind you of another thing. Just because a person joins your church, is baptized, is on the roll, and attends church does not mean that he has a personal relationship with Jesus Christ. When you are discipling, one of the first things you will want to discover is what that person's relationship is to Jesus. A person will never grow in the Lord until he has a personal relationship with Jesus Christ.

One semester, as I was listing these marks of a disciple, I said to my class, "Are you teaching your children who have made professions of faith to be disciples?"

Several weeks later one of my students came to me and said, "During class that day I thought of my teenagers and how they are in church every service, but as I began to look for that sweet, personal, daily relationship with the Lord, I could not find it in their lives.

"I began to look for other marks of a disciple," Jim continued, "and I realized that I was not building *disciples*. I was building *'churchgoers.'* "

Immediately, Jim began to intercede for his teenagers. He prayed, "Father, help me to be the kind of father that will help my children become disciples of Jesus Christ. Let them see the characteristics of a disciple in me."

Jim continued, "Several weeks passed. One Sunday night after the service my fourteen-year-old daughter came to me, put her arms around me, and said, 'Daddy, I want you to know that Jesus has not been real in my life. I want a personal relationship with him like you have. Can you help me?' Now all of that stress and strain between parent and child has dissolved."

As you are going, you should be careful *never* to disciple people to yourself. Instead disciple them to the Lord Jesus Christ. Because if you disciple people to yourself, they will try to *imitate you;* therefore, they may become very frustrated because they may not have your spiritual gift. They are to bear the *character* of *Jesus Christ* through *their personality.*

I am not Billy Graham. I do not plan to be. When I was a young preacher, I wanted to be a young Billy Graham. But my pastor said, "Oscar, you are not Billy Graham." I was so disappointed.

While I have been teaching at the seminary, I have been interim pastor at many churches. I was called to a church whose pastor had just resigned. I consider this man to be one of the finest biblical expositors in the world today. We are very close friends. But I was going to follow him. Well, I know who I am and I know who he is. Someone said, "Isn't it going to be difficult to fill the other pastor's shoes?"

I replied, "I do not intend to try. They will not fit. I am Oscar Thompson. The people will have to accept me as I am, and I am comfortable with the gifts that God has given me. He is sufficient in me."

I am me. I accept me the way I am because God made me. If I can bear his character in my personality, I am comfortable with that. I do not have to be jealous of *anyone.*

Pastor, do not be intimidated when you follow after a great man of God. Do not be threatened by him or jealous of him or his ministry or the love of the people at the church for him. If you are, your ministry will be greatly hindered; and you will not be able to do what God intended. It is only natural that when a man of God leaves a church, the people will love him and continue to love him and talk about him. That has nothing to do with you or their love that will grow for you. You just be you and allow the Lord to live in and through your life, and people will love you too.

A Disciple Is Under the Total Authority of the Teacher

Being under the total authority of the teacher means that a disciple becomes the personal property of the Lord. It means that you allow Jesus to become Lord of your life. You become Christ-centered. Your life becomes a channel through which God moves and loves and reaches out to people and meets their needs.

You will find the scribes and the Pharisees and others questioning the authority of Jesus, but only once do you find the disciples questioning his authority. The disciples asked him questions and often did not understand what he was saying, but they did not question his authority except one time. Do you remember in Matthew 16:21-23 when Jesus was telling his disciples that he was going to die and Peter said that he was not? Jesus turned to Peter and said, "Get behind Me, Satan!"

A Disciple Possesses and Demonstrates the Character of the Teacher

For a disciple to possess and demonstrate the character of the teacher is essentially what we discussed in chapter 10, "The Real Purpose of Life." It is the concept of our bearing his fruit, his life, his ministry, his love in our lives. The fruit will always reproduce the character of the seed, the seed being the Word of God, the very character of Christ. Galatians 5:22-23 will be demonstrated in the life of the believer.

Remember that Matthew 13:18-23 is the parable of the sower and explains the hindrances to bearing fruit: (1) stolen seed, (2) shallow seed, (3) choked seed, and (4) good seed.

As we discussed, the results of bearing fruit are found in John 15: upward—answered prayer; inward—joy; and outward—love. *Love is meeting needs.*

A Disciple Must Be Prepared to Suffer for the Teacher

Daniel 3 gives us a picture of true discipleship in the midst of suffering. Here Shadrach, Meshach, and Abednego are told that if they would turn from their God and worship the king's golden image, they would not be cast into the fiery furnace.

Shadrach, Meshach, and Abednego replied,

O Nebuchadnezzar, we do not need to give you an answer concerning this. If it be *so*, our God whom we serve is able to deliver us from the furnace of blazing fire; and He will deliver us out of your hand, O king. But *even* if He *does* not, let it be known to you, O king, that we are not going to serve your gods or worship the golden image that you have set up (Dan. 3:16-18).

We need to come to the place where we are ready to say, "Father, whatever it costs me, wherever it leads me, I am ready. I am yours. I am going to be faithful even to death." God has not asked most of us in this country, in this day and time, to be faithful even if we have to die for our faith. But we must be willing. The time may come when we will have to make that decision.

Are you a disciple? I do not know what kind of valleys—disappointments, sorrows, or pressures—the Lord is going to let you walk through. But a disciple knows that he is in the hands of his Lord, that nothing can come into his life except by God's permission, and that God will always provide the strength for whatever comes. A disciple can walk through any circumstances in the victory of our Lord.

Discipleship

Parents, are you building characteristics of disciples into your children? If you are, you will be much blessed. Are you preparing those youngsters running around at your feet to become disciples, or are you just trying to raise some kids?

If all you have done is raised, educated, and kept your children out of trouble, something is missing in their lives. You are to disciple them. Some of your children may be far from God, and that hurts you. But never lose the hope that someday they will become disciples. Pray for it. Also, remember that they need to see that Jesus is real in your life.

Sunday School teacher, look closer at those people—big or little—in your class. What is your obligation when you teach them on Sunday morning? You are to be discipling.

Outside the home, the greatest discipling organization in the world is the church. Pastors and staff members, are you discipling? Are you teaching the members of your church to disciple?

A church might be called "the bunch." I realize that is not couched in the most eloquent of words, but "the bunch" gathers on Sunday morning. What do you do with "the bunch"? Do you browbeat or fuss at them? No! You feed them. You love them. You meet their needs.

As you feed them the Word of God, you will find some people surfacing that hunger to become disciples. I tell my students that if they are preaching the Word, the cream will rise to the top. Skim the cream and disciple it. If people are being fed the Word, some are going to have a desire to become disciples. If the seed is sown, some of it will germinate.

In our Concentric Circles, everyone has a Jerusalem, a Judea, a Samaria, and a world. Jesus said to start where you are and move forward. Where are you now? Where are you going? Jesus told us to make disciples. Are you?

12
Things I Have Learned

(This chapter is from a letter which Oscar Thompson wrote to cancer patients.)

God's purpose in creating people was to have a vehicle in which to reproduce his life and character. Since Adam, this plan has been thwarted by rebellion and sin. But the miracle of God's redemptive love restores people to a relationship through which God's purpose may be accomplished. He uses every circumstance of life to fashion his children into vessels through which he can pour his love and grace. The following is but a brief glimpse of his working in my life.

In 1976, while on the way to the Southern Baptist Convention in Virginia Beach, Carolyn, Damaris, and I stopped in Washington, D.C. for some sight-seeing. That evening I experienced excruciating pain in my right hip. I was taken to the hospital, sedated, and later flown home and hospitalized with a preliminary diagnosis of a slipped disc.

Weeks passed while I lingered in traction, alas, to no avail. In desperation, a spinal fusion was performed. Another two months passed with no relief. Two months later exploratory surgery was performed on the hip.

After surgery I was advised that an inoperable malignant tumor had grown out of the bone. A bone scan later revealed that the malignancy had metastasized and spread to my foot, knee, hip, rib, shoulder, and cranium.

After the doctor left my room that night, a deep, sweet

peace from him who is our peace surged within me. It was simply
inexplicable and ineffable. I reached for my New Testament on
the nightstand and said, "Father, if I am not going to live, I want
to count. I need a word from you." There surfaced in my mind a
passage of Scripture that I had memorized years before. "Blessed
be the God and Father of our Lord Jesus Christ, the Father of
mercies and God of all comfort; who comforts us in all our affliction so that we may be able to comfort those who are in any affliction with which we ourselves are comforted by God" (2 Cor.
1:3-4).

"Oh, Father, I understand. You are going to send me
through the valley so that I can comfort others with your comfort
when they walk there."

Then there came that inner nudge that said, "Read on."
Verses 8 through 11 revealed this promise to my heart:

We were burdened excessively, beyond our strength, so that we des-
paired even of life; indeed, we had the sentence of death within ourselves in order that we should not trust in ourselves, but in God, who
raises the dead; who delivered us from so great a *peril of* death, and will
deliver *us,* . . . you also joining in helping us through your prayers, that
thanks may be given by many persons on our behalf for the favor be-
stowed upon us through *the prayers* of many.

I put down the Testament, rejoiced in the Lord, and later
slipped into a peaceful refreshing sleep. Was I rejoicing because I
felt I would live? No! I was rejoicing because it really did not matter. My life was under his control. I rejoiced because of a wonderful awareness of his love. Verse after verse that I had memorized
began to surface. First John 4:18 exploded in my consciousness.
"There is no fear in love; but perfect love casts out fear, because
fear involves punishment, and one who fears is not perfected in
love."

I knew that nothing could come into my life without God's
permission. If it came with his permission, then I knew that it

surely came with his grace to deal with it. Living and dying is not
the issue of existence, but whether he is permitted to reveal his
character and life in me.

The joy of living is permitting God to do through us whatever he has in mind for each day. Most people's lives are crucified between two thieves, yesterday and tomorrow. God can
only give forgiving grace for yesterday. He stores no provision of
grace for tomorrow. Tragically, most of us live in yesterday and
tomorrow, in that devastating land of "What if?" God has adequate grace to deal with yesterday if it is put in his hands. But his
grace is poured out one day at a time. The person who has not
learned this will never live victoriously. He will always be vulner-
able to circumstances. In other words, *I learned that God does
not give dying grace on nondying days.* To worry about tomorrow is futile, as well as sinful. It occupies my time and mind with
things God did not intend, thwarting his grace and power in my
life.

Today, God is permitting me to teach a thousand young
seminarians how to share their faith. He is also permitting me to
be the channel through which he is comforting those who walk
the painful valley of cancer.

My doctors tell me that I am "incredibly normal again." I am
not rejoicing that I am well again so much as I am rejoicing in the
glorious fact that Jesus is Lord. I can boldly say with the apostle
Paul:

Yes, and I will rejoice. For I know that this shall turn out for my deliver-
ance through your prayers and the provision of the Spirit of Jesus
Christ, according to my earnest expectation and hope, that I shall not be
put to shame in anything, but *that* with all boldness, Christ shall even
now, as always, be exalted in my body, whether by life or by death. For
to me, to live is Christ, and to die is gain. But I *am* to live *on* in the flesh,
this *will* mean fruitful labor for me; and I do not know which to choose.
But I am hard-pressed from both *directions,* having the desire to depart
and be with Christ, for *that* is very much better; yet to remain on in the

flesh is more necessary for your sake. And convinced of this, I know that I shall remain and continue with you all for your progress and joy in the faith, so that your proud confidence in me may abound in Christ Jesus" (Phil. 1:18-26).

PRAISE HIM

CONCENTRIC CIRCLE SURVEY

I. SURVEY

NAME_____

ADDRESS_____

PHONE_____

RELATIONSHIP_____

MARITAL STATUS_____ SPOUSE _____

FAMILY MEMBERS_____

II. INTERCESSION: (MATTHEW 18:19)

PRAYER PARTNER:_____ PHONE _____
SPECIFIC PRAYER REQUEST — NEEDS —

LOVE IS MEETING THIS PERSON'S NEEDS

SPIRITUAL NEEDS:_____

_____

_____

PHYSICAL, EMOTIONAL AND MENTAL NEEDS:_____

_____

III. BUILDING BRIDGES

BIRTHDAY_____

ANNIVERSARY_____

OCCUPATION_____

HOBBIES_____

STRATEGY_____

PASTOR'S NAME_____ PHONE _____

IV. CONFRONTATION: (SEED SOWING)

STRATEGY   **DATE**   **DATE**

PRESENT NEED:_____

_____

_____

_____

CHRIST'S PROVISION:_____

_____

_____

_____

APPEAL_____

_____

_____

_____

V. DISCIPLESHIP: (FOUR MARKS OF THE DISCIPLE)

PERSONAL RELATIONSHIP WITH CHRIST

UNDER TOTAL AUTHORITY OF CHRIST

BEARING THE CHARACTER OF CHRIST

PREPARED TO SUFFER FOR CHRIST